Dr. Ash & Sons

David Ash

22 / 07 / 11

Dr. Ash & Sons
Amazing Inventions
& Crazy Adventures

A story of faith

David Ash

Snakestone

British Library Cataloguing–in-Publication Data

ISBN 0-9550857-7-2

Snakestone is an imprint of
PujaPower Publications

www.snakestone.org

To Ma

On her 90th

Other titles by David Ash:
The Tower of Truth
Science of the Gods
The Vortex: Key to Future Science
The Cosmic Vortex
Science of Ascension
The New Science of the Spirit
Activation for Ascension
God the Ultimate Paradox
Is God Good?
The Power of Puja
The Power of Physics
The New Physics of Consciousness
The Role of Evil in Human Evolution
If The Truth be Known
The Science of Super Energy
Physics of the Quantum Vortex

Acknowledgements
Thank you gracious Àine Faylore for encouraging me to write this book and inspiring the title and thank you Jack Lemmer; with your 102 year old heart full of generosity and loving kindness, you cared for me while I wrote it.

Contents

Introduction

My father was an amazing man. An amateur pioneering scientist in the Victorian mould, he was a doctor, inventor, philosopher, physicist and geologist but also an accomplished healer and dowser. Pa, as we always called him, also practiced osteopathy and acupuncture. He was offering natural therapies in Harley Street decades before alternative medicine became fashionable. He never joined the National Health Service nor did he believe in drug medicine. Making his own homeopathic and herbal concoctions he had more faith in herbs than pharmaceuticals.

A ruggedly independent individual, free thinker and ingenious inventor Pa fitted the role of neither G.P. nor researcher. To picture him imagine an alchemist weighing his potions in drammes and scruples rather than a clinician or scientist in a white lab coat. Pa was more metaphysician than physician, more medicine man than medical doctor. Ahead of his time yet from some bygone era he was ageless; as much at ease treating Native Americans on reservations in Canada as wealthy patients at his fashionable consulting rooms in London

Pa had the courage to proclaim his truth, regardless of opposition. He attracted derision from the press when he first suggested cigarette smoking caused lung cancer. I remember him saying to me when I was a boy: "Even if you find yourself standing alone against the entire world it does not mean you are wrong!"

My father moulded me and my brothers and sisters after his own fashion. He engendered in us a passion for fundamental research. As a member of the endangered species of amateur scientist, he set us on course digging for the diamonds of discovery, not for money or a career, nor to make a name, but for the sheer joy of the search.

I took it for granted that I had to set out and make discoveries. That I might need proper research facilities, grants or expensive laboratories never entered my head. Pa had always managed without them. His medical practice was his source of funds and Ma's kitchen was his laboratory.

As a youngster Pa warned me against expert opinion. He expounded, "Experts cannot be trusted; they are paid hacks!"

He reckoned professors were political lapdogs and had a low opinion of professional scientists. He practiced medicine for a living and that was his profession but his passion was his unpaid research. He used his professional income to fund groundbreaking science. Not only was he the first doctor to speak out about the link between smoking and lung cancer but his research first revealed the link between cancer and radioactive rock lying deep below the ground in Devon and Cornwall.

Pa was the first doctor to speak out about cigarettes and cancer not because he was the first to discover the inconvenient truth but because no one could cut his funding for telling it. And that was the truth he lived. He said, "Only the amateur who works for love and not money can be free of corruption".

Pa encouraged me to follow his footsteps in science but he was emphatic that I should fund my research from a health care practice, as he had done, rather than join the ranks of scientists funded by university grants. "The truth is attracted to love not money," he once told me, "If you want to discover the truth you must do it for the love of science not the love of money!"

On another occasion he commented, "Back me and I go into reverse."

Pa's icon was Ernest Rutherford. He told me how Rutherford discovered the proton and nucleus of the atom with very simple and inexpensive apparatus. He supported his research from his teaching income not a government or industrial grant. He explained that the greatest scientific genius in history worked as a patent clerk. No one paid Albert Einstein to develop the theories of relativity or establish quantum theory.

Pa commented prophetically, "You mark my words David, the more money they throw at physics the less they'll discover."

I never forgot Pa's comment that truth was like magnetism; it was attracted by love and repelled by money. He would have been appalled at the waste of eight billion dollars on the new particle accelerator in Switzerland and the ridiculous ideas that scientists, paid from the public purse, hope to prove by it.

My research and discoveries are chronicled as well as my father's because it is important he is vindicated. He trained me from childhood to do what I have done. Pa set me on a course to bring the king of sciences into alignment with spiritual truth. I owe it to my father to recall the dialogues I had with him. Sadly he died before I published my prediction of the accelerating expansion of the Universe in 1995. He would have delighted to have seen it vindicated by astronomical observation in 1998.

My father wanted me to prove my ideas through experimental science and he helped me to achieve that goal. I have to tell my story alongside his because my story is his. Without his guiding light I would not have done what I have done.

My brothers and sisters have a story to tell too because they carried on different aspects of Pa's pioneering work. While my focus has always been on physics, Steven continued the healing and natural medicine and Simon followed the direction of practical inventiveness. Jenny took up nursing and Yoga while Mary leapfrogged us all for a while in unbridled shamanism and Peter and Richard maintained his love for the wilds of Cornwall and the rolling ocean swells. Pa hosted the first surf life saving team from Australia that visited Bude and now two of his grandsons are surf champions. The family have carried his vision on and beyond him, each in there own way. This is their story too.

This book is more than a family tale. It is a statement for amateurs everywhere, people with passion, the unpaid pioneers, and men and women of vision who are on fire to do what they do, albeit in kitchens, garages and sheds. The professionals may call the amateurs crackpots and cranks but then as Pa said, "Without cranks engines won't work."

My father's life was a story of faith and more than anything else this book is intended to convey that. It also serves to remind that the indomitable human spirit can never be suppressed. Most important of all, Pa wanted to show that young people everywhere can aspire to change the course of history, alone and unaided; and have a lot of fun doing it. That is my story.

.

Chapter 1
Galloping Horses

It is easier for a father to have children than for children to have a real father.

Pope John XXIII

If you look in the stud books of the *Suffolk Punch* you will see the Pratt family dominated the breeding of this heavy horse. Pratt was my great, great grandfather and he was awarded a medal by the Czar of Russia for breeding war horses. The Suffolk Punch hauled guns into position in the Crimea war and Russian artillery batteries depended on horses bred by my ancestors in the Great War.

My forbears' renown for fine breeding didn't stop at horses, they bred beautiful daughters and granddaughters too. Gorgeous girls with luxurious locks billowing in the breeze rode the stud stallions bareback. Geneticists visiting the stud from far and wide to learn about breeding were attracted by these nubile riders. My paternal grandmother captivated a visiting Russian. No medals were conferred when she fell pregnant. Her illegitimate firstborn went out for adoption. The next bewitched biologist of breeding was Edward Cedric Ash; a farmer and teacher at Cirencester Agricultural College. He eloped with my grandmother, Edith Pratt but they paid the price of religious intolerance. They were disowned by their families because he was a Jew and she a gentile.

Uncle Bob was the first born then my father; Michael – nick named Tim – arrived on October 21ˢᵗ 1916. Finally Jock appeared to complete the family; well not quite. My granddad still had his penchant for fillies and wild oats. My grandmother said there was a time when she felt her home was a maternity ward because he made a habit of bringing back his girl friends when their pregnancy was discovered. Who better to guide them in mothercraft than his own dear wife! Unfortunately she didn't share his passion for diverse bloodstock and felt as though a bucket of fish-water had been emptied over her head each time a swollen eyed damsel in distress arrived for sweet solace and more than a tender embrace. The last one was Barbara.

One day Barbara's mum arrived on my grandma's doorstep to take my grandpa away. My grandmother hid behind the curtains. Determined to make a good woman of her pregnant daughter, the future dragon-in-law persuaded my grandpa to divorce my grandma leaving her penniless with three boys to feed. So poor was she that when someone came selling beetroots all she could afford were the tops.

My grandfather rectified the situation of my grandmother's destitution by placing a classified advertisement in *The Times,* offering her three sons for adoption. Bob was taken by a kindly couple in the North whilst Tim and Jock were adopted by wealthy Suffolk millers by name of Wiggins. The terms of adoption were that my father was to be put through medical school. Thus it was that a sad little seven year was taken from his mother and Michael Ash came to be renamed Tim Wiggins. The Wiggins enrolled him in Bedford College from where he matriculated to St John's College Cambridge and then went on to Guy's Hospital London, where he graduated in medicine. Jock became a miller.

Mummy Pack

Grandpa Ash

Wedding Photograph

Holiday Caravan

Sadly I never got to know my paternal grandfather because he stuck his head in a gas oven. Nonetheless I did get to see the beautifully illustrated books he produced on dogs and spiders. My grandmother showed them to me when I was seven and I have before me, as I write, his book on Farming published in 1928 in which the then minister of agriculture, Lord Bledisloe wrote: *It is from such men as Mr. Edward Ash, in these days of agricultural depression and farming despondency, that we should do well to learn.*

Hearing the stories of my grandfather and reading his book I realise how much of him there is in me. It confirms my confidence in nature over nurture.

I don't think my father ever forgave his sire and he determined to re-establish contact with his mother. After years of searching he located her through Suffolk church records and chatting to local people. The Wiggins disowned him when he changed his name by deed poll from Wiggins back to Ash and for tracking down his mum. I recall following in his delight as he strode up her garden path in Exmouth Devon. She had remarried and taken the name of Packard. Hence we called her 'Mummy Pack'.

Pa brought a pack of little boys back to his mum to replace the ones she had lost. We were the ages of her sons when last she had seen them. My happiest childhood memories were with Mummy Pack because she loved me so much. She taught me to knit and sew and I loved her mangle – a hand operated device for squeezing water out of the washing. She warned me not to get my fingers caught between the rollers as I struggled to manipulate soggy clothes and turn the handle. It was wonderful to watch the water dribble and see the clothes emerge stiffly flattened on the other side of the fearful finger crushing machine. I promised myself a mangle when I grew up but sadly that was not to be; they had been replaced by noisy, hectic spin driers!

I have stronger, fonder childhood memories with my grandmother than my mother; but then that is quite common with children.

So how did my father meet my mother? It all began in war torn Liverpool. Pa was a ship's surgeon and hurrying toward the docks, after a period of leave, he was apprehended by an urchin who asked him to play marbles. Time was short but Pa's intuition told him to obey the child so he stopped for a game. The lad took to his new companion and one game ran into another. Pa told the boy he was late for his ship but to no avail; the child was insistent that he stay longer so Pa went on playing. Suddenly the kid declared, "You can go now!"

Pa ran. He could hear a ship whistle in the distance but reached the port in time to see his merchantman pulling away from the wharf without him. The ship joined a convoy bound for Russia and was torpedoed. All lives were lost. Thanks to the little boy and his marbles Pa survived.

Discharged in disgrace from the merchant navy, Pa was handed over to the army as there was a shortage of doctors in Aldershot. Less than week into his new duties Pa spotted an attractive bottom sticking out of a linen cupboard. As my mum straightened up she knew immediately she was looking into the bearded grin of the man she was going to marry. They snatched the moment and secured an immediate date. That was just as well because Pa didn't last the week in the army.

At sea he had pondered on innumerable problems that threatened the lives in the Armed Forces. One of Pa's concerns was the possibility that servicemen might be delayed at night scrambling to action stations by the struggle to get out of sleeping bags. He solved the problem with the invention of a blanket bag. Pa had stitched together the corners of a blanket to make a bag with holes for the head, arms and feet. To test his idea he made enough for the entire ship's company. Should their sweet dreams of loved ones be shattered by torpedoes, dropping bombs or exploding shells they could kick their hands and feet out of the holes and run to their stations in attire more fitting for lepers than able bodied seamen; but protected from the elements nonetheless!

Despite the fact that the blanket bags didn't save his unfortunate comrades when their ship was torpedoed, Pa was undeterred. He had his own bag to demonstrate and was ideally placed at Aldershot to bring his invention to the attention of the British Army.

Pa believed in direct action. He'd got wind of a meeting between an envoy of Stalin known as the 'Red Baron' and General Montgomery in a railway carriage at Canterbury Station so he hitched from Aldershot to Canterbury and dressed in his bag, paraded up and down the platform outside the supposedly top secret location of a meeting on the second front. The apparition of a Cistercian monk made its mark on the military. The ghostly figure was hauled away by burly M.P.s and dispatched to a lunatic asylum in Dumfriesshire where Pa palled up with a cousin of the Queen and ended up salmon fishing at Balmoral. So there we have it, instead of meeting his maker Pa met Ma and the rest is my history, and that of my bothers and sisters.

Chapter 2
The Nuclear Family

"Truth is magnetic; it is attracted by love and repelled by money."

Michael Ash

Back at sea in the merchant navy my father proposed to my mother in a poem:

> Will you have my David for me,
> David is the sort of chap,
> I want my son to be,
> Bring him up in Cornwall,
> In that cottage by the sea,
> Paddling in the brook for trout,
> And catching prawns for tea.

She accepted with the lines:

> I'll have your David for you,
> He'll grow up by the sea,
> A little, laughing image,
> Of the man I let go free.

Jenny came first bringing to an end parents' holiday in the gipsy caravan. Tim followed sixteen months later. He developed jaundice and was admitted to Great Ormond Street hospital. My father only had access to my mother between his patients and Tim's feed times. One day he collected her from the hospital and took her to a hotel where I was conceived. Strange to say, my first wife was conceived in a London hotel - the Dorchester - four years later. (Not by my father of course!)

I arrived twelve months after Tim. Simon followed me by a mere year and a half - it was Simon who tickled trout for tea. Steven and Mary followed in quick succession. They were born in Cornwall, at St Nectans in Poughill in Ma's Victorian four-poster with an Elizabethan stag hunting scene carved around the frieze. I remember the bed for pushing Simon off it by continually poking him with my peashooter. He broke a collar bone in the fall and I fell from favour in the family for a while.

Peter arrived in 1955 and then after a gap, Richard joined the throng in 1960. I think Pa should have been more honest with Ma and proposed with the line *'Will you have my research team for me...'*

Pa enrolled me and my brothers as his research assistants when we were infants. I was five coming on six when he was researching clusters of cancer in some villages in Devon and Cornwall. He linked cancer to radioactivity and believed uranium in the rock below the houses was responsible for the high levels of the disease. He needed to confirm the presence of uranium in the types of rock shown on the geology maps under the suspect villages and took us out with him prospecting for uranium.

I recall one Saturday morning when Pa packed us into his 1920's Rolls Royce and took us on a uranium prospecting expedition. It was a typical outing for seven dwarfs. Jenny was eight and Tim seven. I was six and Simon only four. Stephen was three and Mary was a babe in arms. She was left behind because Pa's research assistants had to be able to toddle before they were allowed to dig for uranium. Despite her howls her place was taken by five year old cousin Andrew who was staying with us at the time.

Armed with picks, shovels, and a Geiger counter for detecting radioactivity, to a resounding roar of the Rolls, we set off from St Nectans.

As it was impossible to mine for uranium directly under the cancer-cluster houses Pa collected samples of granite from the edge of the moors similar to that his geology maps revealed under the suspect villages. Again and again he found that where the geology under people's homes matched the granite in which he found uranium there was cancer. Uranium decays into radioactive radon. This heavy, inert gas bubbles up from the ground and collects in people's houses where it increases their exposure to radioactivity, and the risk of cancer. Pa was ahead of his time.

Back in the 1950's the experts didn't take him seriously when he suggested that people got cancer because of uranium in the rock deep beneath their homes. Nonetheless, his discoveries led others to repeat his research and today many families are protected from death and disease by venting the deadly gas from under their homes.

Pa locating uranium through a technique called *radiesthesia*. Using this unorthodox method, akin to dowsing, he could home in on a lode of uranium from twenty or thirty miles away; and he taught us how to do it too.

Radiesthesia was important for me because it taught me, from childhood, to incorporate the paranormal with the normal. In my life there was no divide between the spiritual and the scientific. For me there was no schism between nuclear physics and natural healing, no dichotomy between swinging pendulums and clicking Geiger counters.

As usual, Tim sat in the front seat. He had a small sample of uranium rich granite in one hand. With the other hand he scanned the horizon until he felt a tingling in his finger tips. Pa then drove in the direction of the tingle. At road junctions he would stop and let us all take it in turns to feel for the sensation in our own fingers.

Eventually we found ourselves at Bray Down on the North edge of Bodmin moor. Close to a disused ancient copper mine the tickle had turned to a painful prickle and Tim began to cry. None of us wanted to hold the rock sample any more in case it hurt when only minutes before we had been screaming at Tim to let us have a turn.

Pa stopped the Rolls Royce and pulled out the Geiger counter. Jamming the headphones over his ears, he switched it on and swinging open the heavy car door he leapt out and swept about with the probe. Immediately the instrument went berserk. The strongest signal was right under the roller. Pa had located a radioactive lode in the middle of the road. We took it in turns to listen. Over the road the counter went into a frenzy of clicks and the meter needle on the instrument was swinging to the right, indicating a high level of radioactivity.

The Geiger counter was a very exciting bit of equipment for a six year old scientist. It was associated with famous people in science like Rutherford and Einstein and the clatter in the headphones indicating the proximity of the radioactivity and that was absolutely thrilling. Whilst our friends were playing with sticks and imitation guns and swords, we were mining the stuff used to make the atomic bomb!

Pa rolled the Roller onto the roadside and pulled the tools out of the back. In those days minor roads across the moor were still dirt tracks. He didn't care if it was road or bog. He rolled up his sleeves and began to hack away the surface with a pickaxe. None of us knew any better so we pitched in and attacked that road with a vengeance. Can you imagine it these days, a dad encouraging his kids to dig up the road for uranium?

Jenny suddenly noticed Stephen was missing. She ran off to find him paddling in a small stream. I hit my thumb with a pick and retired from the pit howling. That left Tim, Simon, and Andrew with Pa swinging pick axes and wielding shovels.

Simon and Andrew dismissed themselves from the digging detail to do a bit of prospecting on their own. Tim caught them carrying the precious Geiger counter over the rocks of the old copper working. Simon had the headphones on and was sweeping with the probe. Andrew was holding the instrument studying the movement of the needle. They had located more radioactive rocks which delighted Pa. Afterwards they told me he had broken up a bit of granite with the geology hammer he always carried in a brown leather pouch slung over his shoulder. Simon pulled a bit of broken granite from his muddy pocket. In a grubby hand he held out his prize of radioactive rock with the distinctive black vein of uranium oxide.

Pa wanted to complete the road dig as the signal was strongest there. He was also nervous about leaving his fragile instrument with two small boys. Simon and Andrew, upset at not being allowed to continue prospecting with the Geiger counter, decided to leave him to his dig and explore the ancient copper mine on their own.

Progress was better without a pit full of small boys struggling with oversized implements. Tim stuck with his dad. He was the stalwart son who never left his father to toil alone. I sat in the security of the solid motor car, sobbing with the pain of a throbbing thumb. The nail had gone black but the warm smell of leather lulled me to sleep.

I was woken by the call for lunch. Pa's picnic was an uncomplicated affair. Hunks were torn off a loaf of bread and handed out with pieces of chocolate and withered apples. As for drink, we slurped water in our hands from one of the many springs on the moor. Pa made sure we all washed the radioactive muck off our grubby paws before we ate lunch and drank with them.

By teatime, Stephen was soaking wet from playing in the stream and was crying for his mother. Simon and Andrew were lost. I was curled up in the back of the car in a miserable heap nursing my sore thumb. Jenny was trying to comfort us as well as search for the Simon and Andrew.

Pa and Tim, meanwhile, were pre-occupied with a huge lump of granite they had levered out of the hole in the road. Under Tim's studious attention Pa was smashing it with a sledge hammer. I watched them out of the window. Stephen had fallen asleep with his thumb in his mouth. Jenny eventually found the lost boys and together with Tim they were squatting over bits of broken granite. I ran out to join them. Five pairs of small hands picked up the broken fragments and threw them into a sack. We had uncovered real hot rock. The remaining lump of granite was heaved onto the roadside. Sack and tools were then thrown into the back of the car. Piling in, we headed for home. I remember Pa had to reverse the Rolls Royce quite a long way because the atomic crater we left in the road had made it impassable.

First thing Monday morning the sack was tied up with a luggage label and dispatched by train to Cambridge University for analysis. Those little black bits turned out to be 10% uranium oxide. It never crossed Pa's mind to put a warning on the sack of its radioactive content. God knows how many poor passengers, tending their bikes, got radioactivity up their bums from sitting on Pa's sacks in the guard's compartment. No one bothered about health and safety in those days.

I idolised my dad. As he talked to me about famous scientists, my destiny in science was clear from the earliest age. My mum told me that when I was four one of his patients asked me what I was going to do when I grew up. My reply had been, "I am going to prove the existence of God through science!"

When I turned seven we moved from Cornwall to London; Pa had leased the old Chinese Embassy in Harley Street off the Crown. He rented rooms to other doctors and consultants and hired a butler in tails to open the door to patients who then sat on Hepplewhite chairs in the waiting room, alongside a Steinway piano. It was all very grand.

I have a vivid recollection of a scintillation counter, in his consulting room, with its bank of flashing lights. He always took pains to explain to me what he was doing. I didn't understand much but I became familiar with the terms *alpha* and *beta particles* and *ionizing radiation*.

Though he was years ahead of his time, in his radical ideas; Pa belonged to the era of nineteenth century investigative scientists. Science and discovery were his passion. Earning a living was tedium. The things that really mattered were research and invention. Pushing back the frontiers of knowledge with his own bare hands - that's what my dad was about. Home was my university and Pa was my professor.

Suddenly and unexpectedly our Peter Pan Pa flew us from London to Never-Never Land where we landed among real live Red Indians. Pa had decided it was time for us to experience the wild. He sold his Rolls Royce for ten pounds, disposed of the Crown lease, packed away the priceless antique furniture for shipment to Ontario and cancelled Ma's accounts at *Harrods* and *Fortnum & Mason*.

Tim and I were hoiked out of Westminster Cathedral Choir School and after a BOAC flight and a long train journey, we arrived, with the rest of the bewildered family, on one of the wildest Native American reservations in Canada. The only unseeded reservation in North America, the Wikwemikong village of the Huron nation was situated on a remote peninsula of the Manitoulin Island out in the middle of the Great Lake Huron.

Ma suffered culture shock so Jenny took over as Wendy. We were the lost boys because we didn't have a clue where we were or what was going on. Peter Pan Pa ran off to play with the Indians. He joined the Huron in hunting, and fishing. They accepted him into their tribe giving him the native medicine name for 'Iron Wood' after the mountain ash they used for making their bows. When he eventually left they were so distressed they downed fire water and shot his replacement!

We were scalped. A Huron barber gave us crew-cuts and then we were handed short but powerful bows with the club ended arrows that the Huron boys used for practice but the Native boys were beastly. They were a lot tougher than us and continually picked fights. We were canaries amongst sparrows.

As a nine year old, I vividly recall a group of boys sitting on my ten year old brother Tim while a swarthy little torturer burnt his legs with sunlight focused through a magnifying glass. The game was Indians and missionaries and that was their version of the traditional Huron practice of hanging red hot arrow heads round the necks of zealous Jesuits who were about to be burnt alive. Tim was screaming in agony but rather than go to his aid and risk the same fate, I ran away in tears and hid. Realising I was a coward rather than a hero hurt more than the punches and kicks from the nasty little blighters.

Simon, just turned eight, gave as good as he got and won acceptance with the Huron boys by bloodying a nose so he was invited to accompany them on sorties into the forest. They drank raw maple syrup from the cans pinned on the trees to collect the sap. Encouraged by Simon's success I won a scrap and was accepted as a blood brother. We had to cut our wrists with a knife and rub it on similar cuts the Huron boys made on their wrists so that the blood mingled. There was no AIDS in those days and no one told us about Hep. C. Hiding our fear at drawing blood was all part of the initiation. I could never spit or whistle as well as the other boys, nor throw the tomahawk, but with practice and help from an old Huron I got really good with my bow and after a while could shoot arrows as well as any.

Our furniture eventually arrived in a big wooden crate, including a single Hepplewhite Chair a Queen Anne sofa and the four-poster bed. Housed in colonial style to the tick of the Regency grandfather clock we settled in a large timber frame house overlooking the scenic Manitowaning Bay.

Pa picked up the thread of his research. Inspired by Pierre and Marie Cure, who isolated a fraction of a gram of radium from a ton of uranium ore, he set up a nuclear experiment. He wanted to prove that cigarette smoke was radioactive so he rigged up a cigarette-smoking contraption in the bathroom. The apparatus worked by running water from the bath tap, which drew the smoke from the cigarettes and dissolved it in the water. Pa eventually collected a full bath of water with the smoke from twenty cigarettes. It only remained to evaporate the water. This is where we came in.

The experiment was planned for a Saturday morning when Pa's research assistants were home from school. Ma took to her bed with a violent headache leaving Jenny in charge. As well as Pa she had two year old Peter, the latest addition to the family, in her charge.

Pa and Tim were in the kitchen. All the hotplates were on full blast and as water evaporated they moved the water through a sequence of pans so that elements in the smoke would be condensed into a single pan.

My task was to bring buckets from the bathroom to the kitchen. With Simon and Stephen as my assistants we filled the buckets from the bath and carried them, splash, slosh into the kitchen. We were only little and it was impossible to carry them without spilling water. Mary, then four, was chasing round with two year old Peter and they were getting in the way. They were either attempting to climb up onto the bath or into the buckets to check out what was going on with the exciting experiment until the puddles on the polished wooden floors were sufficient to play in. Jenny did her best to mop up the mess but in the end we were all soaked.

After a while steam became the problem. The house was filled with vapour and everything was damp. As visibility was reduced by mist Pa threw open the doors and windows! His mind preoccupied as it was, didn't think of Canada or winter! He did what he would have done quite naturally in England. Unfortunately it was still March and temperatures were well below zero. Within a short while the house froze. The curtains went solid. Squealing with delight, Peter and Mary were sliding on ice. Stephen skidded and spilt a whole bucket of water, which added to the rink, making matters even better for Peter and Mary.

By the end of Saturday we were frozen, the house was frozen, everything was iced up but we had evaporated a bath of water. It took blazing logs in the two stone fireplaces along with the central heating on full blast to dry out the house. All of Sunday was spent cleaning up the mess. Ma had a classic weekend migraine but Pa managed to scrape some crystals from the last pan and first thing on Monday he sent them off to a lab in Sudbury, Ontario for analysis. He was delighted when he found out the crystals were radioactive. But his spirits were dampened when the analysis compared with the natural radioactivity of the tap water in that mineral rich part of Canada. Undaunted, Pa continued his research. For me the results were not important; it was the early experience in experimental science that mattered.

David & Simon

Pa's Nuclear Research Team

Mary & Jenny

Jennifer, Tim, David, Simon, & Steven

Chapter 3
Healing Hands

The gift of healing is not given away with medical degrees. It is not restricted to any particular faith. Like the gift of sunshine it comes to the just and the unjust alike, be he layman or physician.

Michael Ash

In the Sioux Native American tradition the bear is the animal of healing and in his build, his temperament and his hugs I remember my father as a bear. He was also a healer. One of my most vivid childhood memories were my father's healing hands. As a medical doctor he used his sensitive, gifted hands over his patients rather than prescribing them drugs. He also used his healing hands on us when we were hurt.

We were living in Harley Street when Pa first introduced me to the strange, magical 'Odic' force of healing he was working with. I recall him building instruments out of wires, coils and condensers in an attempt to measure and amplify this healing power. He taught us how to build a 'cat-whisker' radio set out of a coil, variable condenser and a crystal then he showed us how he could measure his healing power with the same coils and condensers. He said it was a form of electromagnetic radiation similar to radio waves. For that reason when he spoke to us he referred to his healing ability as 'radiation'.

I have a vivid childhood recall of him building a balsa wood wheel, balanced on a needle, with little paper cups dangling from silk threads at its periphery. Pa's *Rotary Electroscope*, as he called it, was like the carousel of chairs at fairgrounds. He made it spin with the power emanating from his hands. In answer to my incessant questions my father told me all about the Odic force and he wanted me to study science so I could validate his healing ability as a scientific reality. He told me that was possible because, "The power involved uses the healer merely as a channel, they are only instruments."

My father also spoke of radiesthesia to describe his healing power. He belonged to the *Radiesthesia Society* in London. There he met other doctors and scientists interested in the study of healing. As children, he taught us the practice of radiesthesia and encouraged us to heal each other.

The radiesthesia healing procedure was simple. We would hold our hands over a site of injury, three or four inches above the skin and waggle them round; that's why we called our dad a 'twitch doctor'. After a short while we would begin to feel a tingling in the finger tips which sometimes became a prickle. The patient – or victim as we preferred to call them – would report a tingling sensation or a feeling of warmth or cool in response to the healing. Pa taught us to keep going until the tingling reached a peak and then suddenly dropped away.

Pa was very strict with us when it came to healing. We were told we weren't allowed to touch the patient and we always had to rinse our hands immediately after. He said there was a danger of picking up things we were treating if we didn't wash away the residual energy with water.

He also insisted we remove watches before healing as the power could stop mechanical watches; or start them if they had stopped for no particular reason. None of us had watches until our teens so that instruction didn't matter when we were boys. Even today I remove my watch before healing someone and religiously rinse my hands afterwards.

I have a vivid recall of an experiment in radiesthesia I conducted with Pa when I was in my teens. We were living in Sussex on the south coast of England at the time. Pa had called on my assistance to record the effects of his healing at a distance. A professor in Texas had a child with leukemia and had written to my father asking for healing. Pa agreed but asked the scientist to record the effects of the healing on the boy. Pa also obtained a blood spot from the child on a handkerchief. He asked me to stretch one of my guitar strings on a wooden board and fasten it with staples. Under the string we fixed the measuring tape from Ma's sewing basket with drawing pins. Pa fixed the hanky to the board with thumb tacks and put the end of the wire into the blood spot.

Treatment commenced every morning at eight o'clock or thereabouts. Ma was already up getting the others ready for school. When I poked my head round the bedroom door Pa would be sitting up in bed, meditating on the list of patients he was healing at a distance. As soon as I was set up with my board, watch and notebook he would switch his attention to the Texan child. Sometimes I arrived at eight o'clock and sometimes at ten past eight. Pa preferred my time to be irregular for his experiment so occasionally he would call me up at seven thirty and some mornings he announced there was no treatment. If ever I could delay leaving for college he was delighted; then treatment would commence at nine or thereabouts.

My job was to keep an account of the time the treatment started and when it stopped. Pa also required me to feel along the guitar wire for a tingling sensation before and after the session. I was required to note the distance of the tingling out from the blood spot. What I noticed was that before healing the sensation was a lot closer to the blood spot than after. To begin with it moved from the four centimeter position to thirty centimeters or thereabouts. With time the start distance was ten and sometimes up to fifteen centimeters and then expand to thirty in the course of treatment, lasting anywhere between five and fifteen minutes. Pa randomised the time and duration of treatment.

In Texas the American professor woke up religiously at night in response to any disturbance in his child's sleep. This varied from restless tossing and turning, to crying. He arranged a device to trigger an alarm in his bedroom when the toddler became restless in his sleep and a microphone, amplifier and loudspeaker to wake him from sleep immediately the infant made any discernable sound. True to his word the scientist recorded the time, duration and nature of the disturbance.

When his records were mailed to us and compared with my notes the disturbed sleep patterns in the early hours of the morning in America tallied with the time and duration of the treatments at our end. Allowing for the time difference between England and Texas, my father's meditation on the child and its response was instantaneous. The experiment lasted for six weeks. At the end of the treatment the little boy was found to be clear of leukemia.

What fascinated me about the experiment was the way my father's healing was transmitted half way across the world without any loss of intensity. The treatment was as effective on the child in Texas as if he were in Pa's consulting room in England. That defied all the known laws of physics in regard to electromagnetic radiation.

I was also intrigued that the signal was unaffected by the curvature of the Earth. I realised from this experiment that we were not dealing with a normal form of electromagnetic radiation. I would have to probe deeper to understand what was going on.

There was another aspect to my father's healing power that was even more intriguing. He had, what we called, 'X-ray vision'. When Pa was healing he could see what was going on in the patient's body. The best instance I can recall of this occurred when my dad worked with a patient who had been diagnosed with a tumor on the lung. X-rays had revealed it as malignant and he was booked for surgery. Pa asked me to focus my attention on the patient who wasn't with us but who I happened to know. As I held the focus my father described what he saw in the lung. In the process of the healing session he said he could see the tumor contracting from malignant to benign. He began to describe it as a lump the size of a pigeon egg connected to the lung tissue with a single strand. My dad said all that was needed was for the cord to be severed and the lump to be removed.

When the patient went in for surgery the surgeon was amazed to see a benign tumor, the size of a pigeon egg, in place of the malignancy that had appeared on the original X-ray and in the biopsy. The shrunken tumour was connected to the lung by a single strand! He was tempted to cut the strand and remove the cancer, leaving the lung intact but for the sake of caution decided to remove half the lung.

I was amazed at the power of Pa's healing. His ability to transform a tumor from malignant to benign, and at a distance, was extraordinary. But then my father was an extraordinary man. Watching him, I witnessed many occurrences of healing akin to stories in the Bible. They were nothing short of miraculous. One incident in particular stood out in my mind. We were sitting round a campfire and making tea from water boiling in a makeshift kettle constructed out of a baked bean tin. In the process one of my brothers spilt the entire can of boiling water over his leg. The scald was severe but Pa applied healing immediately, moving his sensitive fingers over the site of injury, three or four inches above the wound. Within minutes tears subsided as the pain diminished and I watched as the angry red in the skin receded. A large blister of fluid was left on the leg but within a day or two this was gone and fresh pink skin had taken its place. What impressed me was under my father's hands, healing that would normally take hours or even days, occurred within minutes.

I had an incredible upbringing and was introduced to more things as a child than most people would experience in a life time. The supernormal was part of my everyday reality. It was only natural for me to endeavor to explain in science things that seemed natural and normal to me in my everyday life. I found it extraordinary that people should question paranormal reality. It all seemed so natural, normal and obvious for me. Such is the importance of upbringing. So much of what we believe has nothing to do with what is. It has more to do with the way our minds are formulated in childhood; hence Jesuits would say: *Give me a child from naught to seven and you can keep the man.*

My unusual father gave me an unusual childhood. The reality I resonated with was the reality he projected when I was impressionable; and his world was a world in which physical and non physical realities existed side by side. My dad often spoke about the scientist, Dr. Wilhelm Reich who invented *Radionics*. Pa worked with radionic machines constructed out of the coils and variable condenser much like our 'cat-whisker' radio sets.

Pa said Reich believed there was a primordial cosmic energy which could influence weather and heal people. My dad explained that the circuits in Reich's radionics boxes were designed to resonate with what Reich called *Orgone energy* and what he called *radiesthetic energy*. As well as his small boxes of isolated circuits Reich designed a box big enough to sit in, intended to concentrate what Pa also described as his 'magnetic energy'.

Pa had one of Reich's boxes in the basement at Harley Street. We used to play in it. It was a sort of Wendy house made of alternating layers of metals and insulators. Reich believed that sitting in the accumulated orgone energy inside the box provided a treatment for cancer and other illnesses. Pa confirmed this in his research. He told me he found his orgone accumulator helped his patients to heal. It certainly packed us full of energy when we played 'Peter Pan' in it. Our nanny found it difficult to get us to stop playing and go to our beds which we then bounced on like trampolines.

My father later told me Reich asked Einstein to test his orgone accumulator. Einstein managed to raise the temperature of an object in the box without a heating source and said the experiment would be a bomb in physics. However, when a professional physicist from Princeton University was called in, the expert dismissed the results saying they were due to convection currents. Pa said the physicist then persuaded the elderly Einstein to dissociate from Reich who had already been labeled as a quack.

Pa repeated the experiment successfully. He said because there was nothing in the box to generate heat the convection currents were a consequence of the temperature rise caused by orgone energy. Even as an eight year old, standing by the box with my Indian headdress and bow and arrow, I could understand why Pa called experts idiots!

Pa said Einstein should have stuck by his experimental findings rather than go along with the skeptic. He said scientists were ignorant when they ignored things. That made sense to me. From the way Pa talked I began to associate the words 'expert' and 'skeptic' with men who ignored or dismissed things or real interest and importance.

Pa fared better in England than Reich in America because he was a fashionable doctor in Harley Street at the top of his tree. He was even on the verge of appointment as physician to King George VI. This came about from an incident on a train.

Pa was sitting in a First Class carriage opposite the Bishop of Rochester who he knew from a healing conference. As he leant forward, chatting to the Bishop, his hands were gesticulating inadvertently above the cleric's injured knee.

The Bishop had hobbled onto the train. When he got up to leave he found the pain in his knee was gone and he could walk without his cane. He wasted no time in contacting Buckingham Palace to announce his discovery of a Harley Street man with remarkable healing powers. After months of vetting and formalities a meeting was arranged with the King and Queen. Sadly a crucial letter of security checking had failed to arrive so the meeting was postponed. Before the second date came round the King had died and so it was Pa missed the greatest opportunity of his medical career.

For Pa, disappointment was a way of life. He took it all in his stride with good humour, "When Kings die in the care of physicians, heads have been known to roll!"

While he was in America things were different. Like Reich, Pa was persecuted. It happened through a prosecution launched against him.

Cornwall

Tintagel

Crackington Haven

Bossiney

St Nectans

Canada & USA

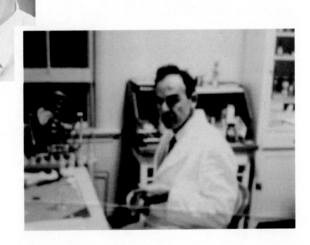

Pa did healing on someone sent by the authorities to trap him. Fortunately he was acquitted because his defense attorney convinced the court that healing was not medical practice.

My father lived by his faith and it never failed him. My mother told me a story from their early days of courtship just after the war. They were hitchhiking in France and ran out of money. Pa went for a pee by a tree and swinging on a branch in front of his nose was a purse full of cash. On another occasion he took my mother for a weekend break on the Great Lakes in Canada. They ended up on a beach on the Canada side of Lake Huron from where they could see the shore on the USA side. In the middle of the lake a small boat was anchored. Three people were on board fishing.

As the afternoon drew on Ma asked where they were going for the night. Pa had no plans. Everything was left in the lap of the gods. Fortunately the gods didn't let him down. As Ma began to scold, Pa drew her attention to the boat that was now speeding across the lake toward them. It beached and two men leapt out shouting for help. They had a boy on board who had gashed himself with a gutting knife. He was white as a sheet and there was blood everywhere.

The men were frantic. They asked my parents if they could get the boy to a doctor. My father had already pulled off his shirt and was ripping it into bandages as he told them he was a doctor and his wife a nurse. Within seconds the flow of blood was staunched, the wound bandaged and Pa was applying his healing to accelerate recovery. Ma cradled the lad in her arms to help him recover from shock.

The two men insisted that their benefactors return with them to the other shore as the boy's grandfather would want to meet them. As they sped across the lake they were told that he was a multi-millionaire who doted on the child.

Alighting on the shore of the USA, Ma and Pa were taken up rolling lawns to a mansion house on the lakeside where they were introduced to Alker Seltzer. When the grand old man heard how they had saved the boy's life he was overcome with emotion and insisted they stay the night as his guests. They were taken up to a luxury suite where three brand new shirts were laid out on the bed for Pa. After indulging in a hot bath they joined Mr. Seltzer for dinner followed by an evening of brandy and cigars in front of a log fire. The following morning, after a hearty breakfast they were taken back across the lake to the spot they had left.

Ma said nothing as they walked beck to the car. Pa lived his life in providence trusting that his needs would be met. They always were but for my mother living on Pa's faith was a source of continual stress. But then, when has living with faith ever been easy for mothers with children.

I remember another instance from childhood of my parent's faith which occurred when I was ten. After we left the Indian reservations we were traveling through the USA on our way to Newfoundland where Pa could practice as a doctor. Parents pulled into a motel but decided to drive on when they realised they had hardly enough money for the next fill of gas, let alone accommodating a family of seven children in a motel. Driving on down the freeway, tired and hungry, uncertain of the future, we all began to pray.

As we were chanting our rosary beads, Ma spotted a hoarding advertising the shrine of Our Lady of Health Happiness and Peace off at the next junction. Pa took the slip road and headed for sanctuary.

We drove into the shrine and spotted three monks struggling to raise a large slab of marble onto an outdoor altar. Pa, Tim, Simon and I ran over and helped them lift. They were very grateful and welcomed us all as we gathered round full of excitement and relief at release from the car and arrival at a destination.

Noticing Stephen eating a candle intended for the altar, the friars offered us supper. My stomach was knotted with hunger. I remember devouring a hasty meal of bread and soup with the monks beaming down at us all, enjoying the sight of seven starving children eating their fill.

Beds were found and the following morning Father Abbot contacted the major benefactor of the shrine, a millionaire called Mr. McBride who happened to be the owner the Framington motel where we had stopped the day before! His first move was to accommodate us free of charge in an older disused motel.

Mr. McBride had invested in a research project to improve the purification of water with chlorine. When he saw Pa's credentials he offered him a job in the research team and gave him a month's salary in advance. A few days later Mr. McBride moved us into his beachfront cottage at New Port, Rhode Island while Pa was flown to Mexico to meet the inventor of the revolutionary chlorine product. Ma, had respite in luxury while we were fully occupied on the farm.

The fabulous cottage was part of Mr. McBride's estate which included a mansion house full of antiques and a farm housing a herd of prize Guernsey cattle. Jobs were found for us boys, cleaning the stalls and feeding the cows. Tim and Jenny were allowed to help with the milking which was all done by hand. I was considered too young and scatty for the milking parlor.

It looked as if we were going to settle in the USA when quite unexpectedly, a month after we had arrived, Mr. McBride died of a brain tumor.

I have a vivid memory of a cow with a broken leg being dispatched with a sledgehammer to its skull. We had been tending the cow as Mr. McBride had refused to allow it to be put down. The day he died we watched the wretched animal being put out of its misery. The sight and 'splitting melon' sound of that slaughter lives with me to this day.

Pa was also dispatched. Fortunately he had just received the second month's advance salary. We were piled unceremoniously into the Ford station wagon and headed off for Newfoundland; this time with money needed to cover the rest of our journey.

Ma was distressed. But she could not have foreseen that Mr. McBride's misfortune would protect her sons from Vietnam. These real life experiences in my childhood taught me to maintain my trust in the unfolding patterns of life for good and for ill. The upheaval of the trip to America was a disaster from a worldly point of view but spiritually it was marvelous. We all learnt that we were always protected and all our needs would be met. The lessons of the trip taught me and my family lessons we would never have learnt at school.

By example, my father showed me the way of the lone warrior who answers to nobody but his own higher self. It was necessary for me to be schooled for adversity. I had to be taught not to be deflected by opposition. Whatever everyone else thought my dad usually thought the opposite, and quite often he turned out to be right. With challenge there had to be good humour and I watched him laugh and smile in adversity and struggle on even when continually haunted by failure. For me that was difficult. I expected things to go well and when they didn't I got depressed. I was more serious than he; the ability to be happy-go-lucky came with years.

Pa was good at beginning things. He never gave up the war but he tended to flit from battle to battle. He would drop one scheme as soon as another, more exciting one came along. His mind was so fertile he found it difficult to stick with a single project to the end and I was determined not to fall into that trap. For the work I was about to do I would need to learn to persist with a project until its completion. I had to heed the warning of Ralph Waldo Emerson: *The majority of men are bundles of beginnings.*

My father also had a habit of jumping to conclusions without giving ample reasons. His genius was intuitive. Brilliant ideas just popped into his head and he expected other people to understand. Then he wanted to tell everyone about his new discoveries and he had to tell them immediately. He was so impatient to get his ideas across that he would enthusiastically rush off his new inventions half-baked. He thereby made it difficult even for those who wanted to support him. Unfortunately that is my failing too and like my father the trait has worsened with years.

Pa was surrounded by frustrated friends and angry enemies. Many of his tendencies I either acquired or inherited from him. He used to say that I should take him as a warning, not an example. But that was easier said than done when he was my mentor - and I had him in my genes!

After two and a half years in Canada, Parents reached a dead end in Newfoundland. A fire in a riverside cabin we were living in was the death of Pa's dreams of fame and fortune in the Americas.

The fire engines were terrific fun for us boys but Ma's antique pieces of furniture were left out in the rain. Insurance; I don't think that word was in Pa's vocabulary. The Hepplewhite chair, Queen Anne sofa and grandfather clock were auctioned along with the four poster bed. Newfoundlanders in the 1960's weren't renowned for appreciation of antiques so I doubt if they survived; though the couple who bought the bed said they intended to build an extension to their cabin to house it. I imagined it had been sawn for logs.

Pa never achieved money or success - he started on the downward slope after he left Harley Street and I don't think he ever hit rock bottom. But as his finances diminished his faith increased and with his vast family, his rude health and a long suffering but loving wife he was always a happy man. Over the years he slowly mastered the craft of living, which was to enjoy what life gave him rather than grumble about what it didn't. But he continued in the firm belief that fame and fortune were just around the corner. He had his indomitable faith and his hope that things would get better tomorrow and as for charity he would always give me the coat off his back, the shoes off his feet and a bank note when he could ill afford it.

When we arrived back in England, Ma had no home and Pa had no medical practice and no income so he took a labouring job in a timber yard. To begin with we stayed with the Neives who chain smoked 'Woodbines', in the basement of their house in Enfield. Conditions were below basic and so other friends of the family, the Hinksmans, took Jenny and Tim into their care in Bromsgrove. Eventually a dear old vicar called Reverend Hobhouse found us a house to rent in his parish at Bexhill-on-sea, Sussex. This was heaven sent for Ma because her parents were living in Bexhill at the time. She was so happy to be back in England with a new home that she fell pregnant for the eighth time.

Pa found work as a locum doctor in Middlesbrough over Christmas - and I was the lucky little fellow he chose to take with him. It was 1960 and I was twelve. My first experience of locum work was grim. It was night as we approached the outskirts of the city and we were caught in a traffic jam.

A call came up the queue of cars for a doctor and so Pa went striding down the tail back with me hurrying along after him with his medical bag. We arrived at the scene of an accident and Pa was asked by the fire services to certify someone as dead. Whilst he scrambled in the wreckage I was transfixed by a small pool with a pair of false teeth floating in it. Being dark, I couldn't make out if it was oil or water so I stuck the toe of my shoe into it. It shifted like jelly. To my horror I realised it was blood!

On Christmas Eve Pa and I went out on the first call. We entered a dark and gloomy house in which an old person had just died. Staring down at the ashen corpse, I had my second encounter with death.

Because it was Christmas day the guest house in which we were staying closed the dining room so Pa and I had to go without breakfast. We spent all day visiting the sick - that is people who had made themselves sick through eating and drinking too much! Apart from a glass of sherry and some chestnuts no one thought to offer us food or drink. All we got were complaints for not having arrived sooner. On Boxing Day our landlady brought out a plate of turkey sandwiches. That was the first bite to eat I had in two days. Pa had no cash and we couldn't buy food anyway because all the shops were closed. It was a miserable Christmas but it meant a lot to Pa that I was with him.

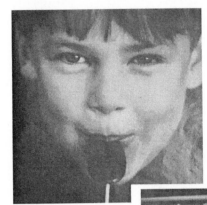

Lollipop Family

Pictures courtesy of LIFE magazine

Chapter 4
Sorcerer's Apprentices

"The more money they throw at physics the less they'll discover"

Michael Ash

The time was 1962. The problem was the Cuban crisis. The threat was nuclear extinction. The solution was lollipops!

With the imminent danger of atomic war, Pa wanted to protect us against radioactive fallout by putting natural minerals in our sweets. Turning fourteen I could comprehend the science behind his idea. It was ingenious. Pa showed me the periodic table of the elements and how it should be possible to use natural minerals to protect against radioactive ones. For instance, he thought it might be possible to use calcium and magnesium to protect against radioactive strontium. Pa expected me to read for myself about radioactive isotopes and the discoveries of Ernest Rutherford and theories of Albert Einstein to keep pace with him.

Pa's immediate action was to add natural iodine to sugar to protect children against the uptake of radioactive iodine. He boiled the iodine enriched sugar into candy then, with our enthusiastic help, he churned out lollipops which we devoured. The concept was a huge success with the R&D team so he offered his recipe for fallout protection to the world. It brought in a wave of publicity which delighted us, but not Ma! In newspapers and magazines worldwide, we were featured sucking our lollipops.

Despite *Life* magazine denouncing Pa's iodized lollipops as ineffective, Americans were so worried by the threat of atomic warfare that they welcomed Pa's initiative. Ours were the first children's faces to be transmitted across the Atlantic via *Telstar*, the world's first television satellite. We were proud when our school friends saw us on *Movitone News* at the local cinema. A girl wrote me a letter from America wanting to be my pen-pal but I wasn't interested in girls so I didn't bother to reply.

For Ma it was mayhem. She had grown accustomed to her kitchen doubling as a laboratory, but not a lollipop factory! All surfaces were constantly sticky and reporters and photographers descended on us without warning. With film and television crews trampling her flower beds Ma's anger erupted. Julian Pettifer got it in the ear because he left one of her tea cups under a hedge.

By 1964, the fallout crisis had blown over and with it the interest in fallout-free-lollipops. In the House of Commons, the Home Secretary buried the invention with the statement: *sweets ruin children's teeth*. As an enterprising fifteen year old my response to the right honourable Quintin Hogg was to fortify the lollipops with minerals to strengthen children's teeth. I had a paper by a Swedish scientist called Alfred Asländer entitled *Complete Tooth Nutrition* and I used his analysis of minerals in teeth, raw sugar and molasses as the basis of my formulation to 'replace into sugar, minerals removed during refining'. I then strengthened the formulation to supplement minerals lost through the processing of other food. That was how I first became interested in nutrition.

Lessons from Pa included not only science but the valuable principles of entrepreneurship. We were each encouraged to set up our own manufacturing and marketing enterprise. We were responsible for everything from production to end sales. We never received any pocket money. If we wanted money we had to go into business. My business was 'Mineralised Sweets'. I remember contacting a firm in the Midlands called Willie Boxes Ltd., and ordering 100 white candy boxes with my own labeling embossed in gold. I was very proud of those cartons. One Saturday afternoon a month I would commandeer the kitchen table to make peppermint creams from my mineralised sugar. I sold the sweets to Pa's patients for ten shillings a box.

Another enterprise was selling ground up seaweed through *Fortnum & Mason* in Piccadilly. I called that product 'Organic Marine Salt'. My labels this time were gold type on a blue background. I just loved gold print alongside black on my labels, but blue was even classier. Pa would send patients into *Fortnum & Mason* with a prescription for my product which also retailed at ten shillings. I sold everything I made for ten shillings because that is what I was paid every week for delivering newspapers. Most of my earnings were re-invested in Pa's inventories!

By the time I was sixteen I had my own lab in a small room used to house the gas boiler. I cobbled a gas line for my Bunsen burner. In my lab I mixed my minerals. I had a small glass phial of pure Selenium. That powerful antioxidant mineral was so toxic I had to keep it in a safe. I remember mixing vanadium and molybdenum in a multicoloured solution and in the process made my own indicator of acidity and alkalinity. Zinc and magnesium, iron, chromium, copper, manganese, iodine and calcium all found their way into my mineral formulations. Pa organised a local chicken farmer to put my minerals into his feed and Tim went into business on his bicycle selling 'Better Eggs' from door to door.

I also ran the family bank which impressed my mother's cousin Sir Kenneth Bond, then financial director of G.E.C. The only millionaire in the family, he put a pound into each of our accounts. Simon, the major investor wouldn't allow me to give Pa credit but then Tim borrowed to buy a radio and went into default so I went bankrupt. Simon seized the only asset which he holds to this day. He has kept that radio in working order – albeit covered in blobs of white paint - for nearly half a century!

My dad also trained me as his patent clerk. He showed me how to type so I could draft his patent specifications. The training was important for me as it taught me how to write scientific papers. I was fifteen when I started writing patent applications. Two years later I visited the patent office in Chancery Lane to file my first provisional specification. There I met a patent agent in a pinstripe suit who gave me tips on patents and trademarks. We were in a lift when he told me 'Biro' was a good trademark because it was simple and non-descriptive, whereas names that attempted to describe the product function were not so good as they were rarely remembered by the public.

While I was being tutored in patent law my father encouraged me to study common law. He then had me draft contracts and participate in some of his negotiations. I was never good at negotiation but it was valuable exercise. My mother wanted me to become a barrister but she didn't have the same hold on me as my father who engendered in me my passion was science.

When I was eighteen Pa introduced me to Dame Kathleen Lonsdale, a retired women scientist who lived round the corner from us. One of the foremost X-ray crystallographers of her day, she had worked at the Royal Institution and Cambridge and had been part of W.H. Bragg's team who developed the X-ray techniques used by Francis Crick and James Watson in the elucidation of DNA.

This wise, elderly lady warned me of the dangers of pollution, food processing and factory farming and spoke to me of soil degradation and non-sustainable agriculture. I told her how my father was a friend of Lady Eve Balfour who founded the *Soil Association*. I also mentioned how three years earlier I had already done a lot of work with my father and my brothers and sisters on a novel way of regenerating the soil through recycled waste. She was impressed by our ecological enterprise and encouraged us to continue with it.

Pa had been on locum in Worthing on the coast of West Sussex. Worthing had a problem. After summer storms seaweed was cast in great stinking heaps all over the beaches. The pong and the flies discouraged tourists. Pa stepped into the Borough Council like the Pied Piper with an immediate solution to the problem. He suggested that the seaweed be layered with sewage sludge and ground-down household waste to make compost for growing mushrooms as Worthing had a thriving mushroom growing industry so there was a local market for the end product. The Council supported the idea. Thus 'Daddy's Dirt' was born.

A local farmer, convinced that the compost was black gold, agreed to have the first heap of Pa's synthetic soil built on his land. Leatherhead Council sent in a lorry load of municipal waste from Surrey, and Worthing Corporation allowed the farmer to take his tractor and trailer onto the beach to collect seaweed. They also sent in a tanker of sewage sludge. When the fleet of smelly plant assembled on the farm Pa supervised the construction of Worthing's first wiffy mountain!

Locums are temporary engagements and Pa found himself back at Bexhill long before the compost was made. His chronic shortage of cash made it difficult for him to get back to Worthing to complete the project. Instead he built a small pile in our back yard! We were marched down to the beach to collect seaweed. Pa located the local source of sewage sludge and Leatherhead Corporation obligingly dumped a truck of ground-down municipal waste outside Ma's front gate. The stinking mound in our back garden was a great success. That was because it was Simon's project. He inherited Ma's practical genes. Simon made excellent compost which he packed into plastic bags and sold, from the back of his bicycle, to retired folk to put on their roses.

Three years later we happened to be driving past Worthing. Pa was optimistic the project had mushroomed in his absence but as we drove up to the farm an ominous black heap loomed in the distance. We went bouncing up to the farmhouse but the farmer set his dog on us. I can remember racing back to the car with it snapping at my heels!

My father wasn't the only party guilty of leaving black heaps on the landscape. On his 50th birthday, the 21st of October 1966, the Pantglas Tip at the Merthyr Vale Colliery engulfed a school at the coal mining village of Aberfan in Wales. In response Pa went on locum to Merthyr Tydfil to champion the use of his synthetic soil to stabilise coal heaps. The Coal Board took the concept very seriously. But then a very different landslide occurred which took Pa's attention right away from growing mushrooms and covering coal heaps. The alcohol breath test became law.

I will never forget that day. I was in Pa's consulting room. Papers on the coal-tip project were spread all over his treatment couch. I was typing a reply to a letter from the chairman of the Coal Board and I needed his help but Pa was miles away.

My father had studied biochemistry at Cambridge University under Professor Sir Gowland Hopkins father of vitamins and Albert Szent-Gyorgyi, who discovered vitamin C, was a demonstrator in his lab. From Szent-Gyorgyi, Pa and his fellow students learnt that the ascorbic acid crystals helped them stand their drinks.

On the day the breath test became law, Pa had two little tablets in his hands. One was a black, charcoal and kaolin tablet and the other was a white, vitamin C tablet. He held them up and ceremoniously pressed them together with glue, proclaiming that he had created the panacea for alcohol.

I suppose I should have felt privileged to have been present at that historic moment but I wasn't. I was very angry. I had put a lot of time and effort into stabilising slag heaps and knowing my father, as I did, all my work was in vain. Once again he was off on another track. He didn't reply to the letter from the Coal Board, indeed I don't think he ever mentioned the subject of coal heaps to me again. Alcohol, the scourge of humanity, was a far more important quest for Don Quixote. As he charged off to challenge the windmills of government I went galloping after him.

Pa had us all convinced that he was going to make his fortune at Christmas. Ma really believed that at long last this was the brain-wave that would pay off all the debts and secure her a steady income. In the spirit of Jenner who first tried his vaccine on a disadvantaged member of his family, Pa tested his 'Alcohol Antidote' on Ma and found that it really worked!

Ma was pruning her roses in the front garden when she was whisked off to the studios of *Southern Television* in Southampton. There she was plied with several double brandies and in an inebriated state she made her television debut.

Have you never seen your mum drunk on telly? It can be a shock if you never even saw her tidily before. We gathered around the television, wide-eyed at the sight of our mother on *Today*, the magazine programme that followed the early evening news. She was sprawled out in a chair, completely incapacitated. All she could do was giggle. A doctor came in with a *Breathalyzer* and tested her. Her blood alcohol level was well over the limit. Pa then came in and administered his pills. After that the local news and other items of the programme continued. Twenty minutes later parents came on again. Pa was interviewed then Ma and she spoke coherently. When breath-tested again the nervous doctor fumbled with the balloon and tube of crystals so they had to do it all again. The next time Ma blew into the balloon she snatched the *Breathalyzer* from him and dexterously slipped the neck of the balloon over the tube. She couldn't have done that if she was drunk. My mother was sober and passed the test, well below the limit. The programme ended with Ma, still in her gardening togs; walking down a white line - arm in arm with Pa - to the strains of the tune ...*I had a little drink about an hour ago and its gone right to my head...*

We were off again. Reporters and film crews were back, trampling on Ma's carefully tended flower beds. Pa had thousands of little black, bullet- shaped pills of charcoal and vitamin C made up. With all the publicity, pubs were crying out for his alcohol antidote. Tim had been selling brushes door to door at the time and so Pa put him in charge of marketing. I headed research and development. I was also expected to be the trouble-shooter and my God was there trouble!

If you are finding this story a bit breathless you can imagine what it was like for me trying to get through my homework at the same time!

The British Government was none too happy about my father's audacious challenge to their brand new breath-test law and set the new *Dunlop Committee for Drug Safety* onto him. I believe we were their first case! I took a day off college and went up to London with Pa when he had to face Dr Denis Cahill, chief medical officer of the Dunlop Committee. I remember the meeting well; it's not the sort of thing one forgets in a hurry!

We arrived at a plush office in Whitehall. The carpet on the floor was red. I recall that because I spent a lot of time staring at it! Dr Cahill did a lot of shouting. We were breaking the law by launching a new medicine without a license. Pa argued. In a stubborn voice he said, "The alcohol antidote is not a medicine; it is a food so we don't need a license. It is nothing more than a mixture of vitamin C charcoal and kaolin. Are you suggesting people need a license to eat oranges and burnt biscuits?"

The face of Her Majesty's Medical Officer flushed as red as the carpet. I wanted to crawl under the large walnut table in the middle of the room when the enraged Dr Cahill bellowed, "Because you described your product as an 'antidote' it is classified as a drug. A substance is considered a medicine not because of what it is but because of what it does! You have claimed a therapeutic action; therefore your product must be withdrawn from the market until it is tested in clinical trials."

Pa contacted the professor of medicine at Guy's hospital who offered to help. I took another day off college to travel up to London and organise the clinical trials. The professor was very accommodating and said he would test the pills so long as they weren't already on the market. I gulped hard and hoped Tim wasn't having much success in selling the pills. Unfortunately, he was. The professor of medicine at Guys had told me to draw up protocols for the trial. I was at home looking up the word 'protocol' in the dictionary when all hell broke loose!

We were a big, disorganised family and Pa left us each to get on with our own thing. He never sat us all down together for a meeting so there was no communication between R&D and marketing. Tim had pressed ahead with the press launch of our product at a pub in Petersfield totally unaware that the double blind clinical trials I was attempting to organise were conditional on sales of the pills being suspended pending results and I didn't know *The Daily Telegraph* had featured a leading article on our pills with a photograph of customers buying the Alcohol Antidote at the bar until an angry phone call from Guys hospital informed me that the trials were cancelled. The phone was red hot that day. I think Dr Cahill read the *Daily Telegraph* over his corn flakes too! Would it be the immediate gallows at Tyburn for Pa or something more drawn out at the Tower?

Pa was not one to be intimidated by the government but when Ma threw a tea cup at him he acquiesced. The Alcohol Antidote went into oblivion but there were plenty of other projects to keep us occupied.

We were living in a Georgian house called Chantry Cottage in the Old Town of Bexhill where Pa had established a small but successful practice in the front rooms. This was now his only source of income.

I did the book keeping but this was frustrated by Ma incinerating the receipts. Periodically she would clear out the house. Anything lying about went on the bonfire. We kept our rooms tidy because we had no way of knowing when the mood might take her to sweep through the house like an avenging angel stoking the fires of hell. Pa lived in the middle of a muddle of papers. Ma never touched them but when I left the box of receipts lying around they went on the pyre. Then a tax assessment for £3,000 landed on the doorstep. There was nothing I could do to challenge it.

A three thousand pound tax demand may not sound a lot these days but when you consider our rent was only two pounds a week, that tax bill was a huge amount of money. The final demand set Ma weeping and gnashing her teeth. I dropped into Armageddon mood. Pa only reacted when she screamed at him he would have to sell his Rolls Royce! He had no intention of doing that. He had only just bought the sleek black Goshawk; she was his pride and joy.

Barely lifting his attention from his typewriter, Pa remarked that as it happened to be the feast day of St. Mark, patron saint of tax collectors, maybe we should go to church and pray to him for help with our tax problems. I wasn't confident prayers would save us and stormed out of the room. I joined Ma in the kitchen over a fretful cup of tea when Pa appeared and insisted I accompany him to church.

I walked in sullen silence beside my father, down the hill and into the Catholic church of St Mary Magdalene. We knelt down to pray. Suddenly Pa leapt to his feet saying he had received instruction to go and speak to the parish priest. I was distraught. I could not get my father to take the matter of taxation seriously. What good would it do speaking to a priest about our tax problems? We'd be off to see the nuns next! Pa ignored my pleas for a sensible approach and strode across to the presbytery. I listened impatiently as our sorry tale was relayed to the thoughtful cleric.

"As a matter of fact I might be able to help you there," the priest said scratching his chin. "I went to school with Jim

Callaghan and we are still friends. If you write out everything you told me in a letter I will send it on with a covering note."

I was still in shock when we arrived home. Pa had told me to write a letter to the Chancellor of the Exchequer! There was no arguing. I was handed the typewriter and a sheet of his letter-headed notepaper and left to it.

After three drafts I perfected an impassioned letter. I impressed the Chancellor with the family research and our financial challenges. I explained that as we were self funded the tax demand would bring a halt to our natural family planning project. I told him of my age and the US patent I had just secured. It was the best letter I had ever written. I handed it in at the presbytery and it was posted to 11 Downing Street with a covering note from the parish priest ratifying the value of our work for the Church.

Pope Paul VI had shocked the world with his condemnation of the pill and artificial methods of birth control. As a catholic doctor, Pa had invented an instrument for detecting minute changes in body electricity between the hand and the vagina that were known to occur at the time of ovulation. It was for this piece of equipment we called 'Ovin' that I secured my US patent. Ornate with the seal of the US Patent Office, it filled me with pride and achievement. All on my own I had completed the full specification with drawings and working detail of the hand held instrument, with its black conductive silicone rubber vaginal probe.

The work, only a part of my father's research into natural family planning, required of me skills normally reserved for patent agents, a rudimentary knowledge of the law, and a detailed workings of the female anatomy. All this was threatened by the taxman! We prayed the rosary for nine days for protection from the Inland Revenue! Our prayer was answered. Jim fixed it for us.

Three weeks later my father received a letter from the Collector of Taxes in Hastings. I went with him to the Tax office. We were ushered in by a short, stout balding gentleman in a neat grey suit. I can best describe his attitude as reverent. After we had been served tea and biscuits we received an apology for the tax assessment. Pa was told that he would never again receive a tax demand as Inland Revenue was suspending his file. So long as he gave them no further trouble, the tax man promised that Inland Revenue would not trouble him again. From that day forward my father never had any tax problems. St Mark would appear to work for those who pray about their taxes!

My other course in Pa's university was public speaking. Whenever Pa was invited to lecture he would send me off to speak on his behalf. I traveled all over the country and quickly developed lecturing skills. I would talk about my extraordinary father, his healing and his research. The ladies loved it but the event organisers were less than happy at the arrival of a lanky teenager in place of the distinguished doctor. Nonetheless for me it was essential grooming for my life to come.

At the same time our soldering skills in the manufacture of Ovin were employed to solder components into the new 'Acuprobe'; an instrument Pa invented for detecting acupuncture points. Acuprobe went on sale in the waiting room alongside the Ovin, Mineralised Sweets, Better Eggs, The Alcohol Antidote and plastic bags of Daddy's Dirt! Chantry Cottage was a hive of industry. The kitchen table was where it all happened and every child had a task, right down to Richard, the youngest.

There was so much going on in my life it was difficult to keep track of it all. I recall a radio interview I had to do on my father's behalf. I had just arrived home from college when Ma gave me an address on a scrap of paper, along with my bus fare and told me to go back to Hastings. The interviewer was asking me questions and I had no idea which invention he was talking about. Into this maelstrom of activity dropped the vortex.

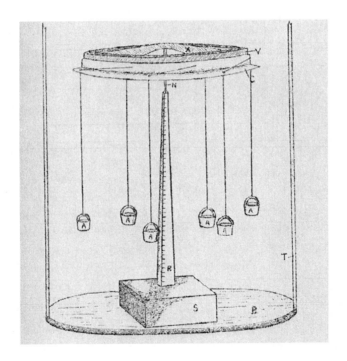

Pa's Rotary Electroscope

Chapter 5
Discovering the Vortex

"You have to swim against the tide to progress with original thought."

Michael Ash

At shy sixteen, sunning myself on the shingle of the Sussex south coast, I noticed a girl looking across at me. Rippling a muscle or two I walked over to her and started to chat.

"You know what," she said, squinting at me in the bright sunlight, "You remind me of an Oxfam advert!"

I enrolled on a Charles Atlas course immediately. But that didn't last. Mary opened one of the envelopes containing exercises and showed it to Ma and the subsequent teasing pulverised the last remaining fragments of my confidence. Fortunately, my school pals were more empathetic.

One late afternoon after school I was jogging on the playing fields with my friends Joe and Chris when Joe suggested, "Hey Dave why don't you try yoga exercises? They might help you put on some muscle."

Chris, who was a yard or two ahead of us, chimed in, "My dad has books on yoga in the attic. If you come back to my place you could have a look."

Chris lived with his family in the top flat above our dentist. Before, I had entered the place of molar torture in trepidation but on this occasion a sense of expectation filled me; an excitement that could not be justified by the mere thought of building up muscle.

I gawped at gaping dentures while Chris dug his dad, a dental technician, out of a room in the back. The spectacled man, in a grimy lab coat handed over a bunch of keys and we bounded up the stairs. Chris unlocked the door and Joe and I followed him into the attic.

It was a musty, airless garret dimly lit by small windows set high in roof turrets but stepping into that attic I crossed a threshold of revelation. I was about to discover a key that would unlock my mind to a radical worldview that could lead me to a complete transformation of physics and reappraisal of the concept of God.

We were confronted with a collection of rare antiquarian books. The walls were lined with shelves stuffed with volumes from the floor to the rafters. Every nook, cranny and crevice was crammed with old tomes.

Chris knew what he was looking for. He pulled two blue books from the shelf. They were pale with age. Blowing off the dust, he handed them to me. One was called *Fourteen Lessons in Yogic Philosophy* and the other; *An Advanced Course in Yogic Philosophy*.

I took the books home and read them avidly. They didn't contain a single exercise to help me put on muscle but that didn't matter. They gave me direction for my life's work, starting me on a journey of discovery, in line with my father's direction, that would occupy me for the next forty five years.

It was a single sentence in the Advanced Course that set the course of my life. As I read it, it seized my attention: 'Energy - *prana* - exists in matter - *akasa* – in the form of vortices – *vritta*. '

Thanks to Pa, I knew enough about Einstein to appreciate the implications of that sentence. Einstein published his epoch smashing equation $E=mc^2$, in an obscure German journal in 1905. Those lessons in Yogic philosophy had first gone to print in the late nineteenth century and were based on teachings that went back thousands of years.

Not only had the Yogis anticipated Einstein, they solved the greatest mystery in physics; describing precisely how energy forms matter.

Even as I write, forty four years after this discover, scientists in Geneva plan to experiment with their new particle accelerator. Probing the atom at vast public expense they hope to resolve the mystery. Yet thousands of years ago mystics in India solved it for nothing. Probing the atom with super normal powers of the mind they discovered how energy forms mass; quite literally they saw quantum spin!

The Yogis went beyond Einstein when they revealed the form of energy in matter to be a vortex; a maelstrom of light. Trained by Pa I recognised that in the old book on Yogi Philosophy I had discovered the most important principle in physics. School didn't help. We didn't do physics at school. Most science lessons were occupied with copying a dictionary of science off the blackboard and the G.C.S.E. examination was an insult to intelligence as was my school an insult to the word education. In my ludicrous science exam I was confronted with an earthworm in a Petri dish and expected to identify if via a multiple choice question paper. By incorrect examination I could have been led to the conclusion that the specimen before me was a tiger. Working backwards I placed ticks from the earthworm to the question.

Nonetheless, I am grateful for the lack of science education at the secondary modern school in which I was incarcerated for five years for the crime of being a child. I was protected from brainwashing. When I started physics at a college of further education in Hastings, I was seventeen, old enough to educate myself in science and configure it into my own framework of understanding.

At college I developed my own wave-particle model for the photon from an interpretation of the theories of James Clerk Maxwell and Albert Einstein and I mixed with a group of stimulating mature students who impressed on me the importance of questioning everything I was taught. An out of work actor in his mid twenties was the leader. He made the deepest impression on me. To Robin Piper the world was theatre; nothing was real. I recall the light in Robin's eyes when he exclaimed, "Everything is abstract!"

In those three words Robin planted an acorn in my mind that would grow into a mighty oak from which I would fashion the strongest plank of my physics.

Words were Robin's profession. He encouraged us to read dictionaries during breaks so as to appreciate their original meaning. He emphasized "Never take words for granted; the labels we impose on things hold secrets that are masked by common usage."

Waving his entomological dictionary at me he exclaimed, "Dig into entomology and you will discover word meanings of real significance."

Thanks to Robin I stopped taking words for granted. As I used them I was on the lookout for their essence of meaning and well as their common value for communication. Might I see a nuance I had not seen before? The word I pondered the most was *energy* because I knew from Einstein that word held the understanding of everything.

Richard Feynman said, in one of his famous lectures, *"It is important to understand in physics today we have no idea what energy is."*

On a wild day in late September 1967 I received an understanding of energy and the vortex. It was a revelation that was fundamental to my understanding of the Universe.

I was eighteen and had just commenced my 'A' level, G.C.E. course in physics. As I wasn't happy to learn physics by rote, I kept interrupting the lectures with searching questions about the underlying nature of reality. I had to know *why* things were the way they were, not just *how* they worked. On the morning of that memorable day the two physics teachers had come in together and glaring at me they exclaimed, "We are not here to answer your metaphysical questions. Our job is to get you through the syllabus in preparation for your exams so from now on interruptions to the lectures will not be tolerated!"

I got up from my seat and stormed out of the physics lab, slamming the door behind me. The beach was only ten minutes away at the bottom of the hill. I ran down in tears. The sun was blinding and the wind howled in from the west.

A cry broke from the deepest recess of my being. Above the crash of waves on the shingle I screamed at the Universe. I had to know the answer. I demanded she reveal her secrets.

Mingled with the mew of the wheeling gulls I somehow knew was my cry had been heard. I experienced a deep sense of peace, a feeling of being bathed in love. Now, decades later, I realise in response to my cry I received a download. In that moment I was given the key to a treasure chest of knowledge. I had received access to the master plan of the Universe.

I didn't see it all at once. Over the next forty years a succession of realizations came from the treasury of knowledge. We all have a right to access to our own heavenly chest of revelation because every part of the Universe contains information about the whole. This is the hologram principle. I am not unique. All I did was to want it hard enough. At that time my desire for an understanding of the

Universe was more important to me than anything else. That was why I accessed it when others didn't; they didn't throw their whole being into the longing for it.

We each have a journey of discovery that is true to us. More than anything it is a discovery of who we truly are. Looking back over the years I realise the search was as significant as the finding; the journey as exciting as the longed for destination; the work more delight than labour.

The unfolding of knowledge that occurred in my life from that day forward has been awesome. I cannot claim it as my own anymore than I can attempt to hold the air that I breathe. One who stands on a mountain summit doesn't own the view. Humans can only express what they discover. Universal knowledge is too vast, too all embracing to be claimed by anyone.

I can only lay claim to the originality of my own personal process of discovery; a process that began back in the physics lab a few hours later while I was waiting for the afternoon lecture to begin. Glancing through a new textbook, my eye settled on a plate at the back of the book. It was a photograph capturing the moment a cosmic ray particle from deep space, smashed into the nucleus of a silver atom in the photographic emulsion, shattering it into pieces. Along with the debris of the collision over a hundred brand new particles appeared, created out of the kinetic energy, the movement of the bombarding cosmic ray particle.

As I stared at the picture it was clear to me that the arrested motion of the cosmic ray particle had been transformed into mass. I was confronted with an experiment that showed particles of matter can be formed out of pure activity. I concluded that what was true for these few particles must be true for all other particles in existence.

I realised mass is a form of movement.

In that moment, as I pondered the picture, before the physics lesson began, I had a lucid flash. I saw energy swirling to form the atomic nucleus. As the energy in the cosmic ray bullet drove through the spinning mass of light in the atomic target it spun off to form new particles of matter.

As I stared at the cosmic ray evidence I felt like Paul on the road to Damascus, or Buddha under the Banyan tree. I was enlightened. Our world is not made of material; it is made of spinning light. Atoms are made up out of particles of movement; particles of swirling at the speed of light.

But how could everything be just movement? How could the whole universe be built out of particles that were nothing but bits of pure activity?

For a moment I was mystified then it struck me. Movement where nothing exists to move is abstract. As I looked intently at that cosmic ray photograph Robin's time-bomb about the abstract exploded in my brains. This hectic world of ours is nothing but thought.

When Robin had originally spoken of the abstract I was confused. At the time I had resisted his ideas. I couldn't understand it when he said there was no reality apart from the abstract. However, in the illumination of that moment his seeds of wisdom germinated in the fertile ground of my young mind. Now, at last I understood him. I was seeing his revolutionary idea of everything being abstract proved by science in a Nobel Prize winning cosmic ray photograph.

The atom is a particle of dream-stuff; what an outrageous thought! In an instant I felt as though I had smashed through the fragile illusion of material; it lay shattered at my feet.

I realised we are all living in a dream. Humanity and history – myself included – are but part of a fantastic flight of fantasy. The evolution of the Earth over billions of years, indeed the unrolling of the entire Universe appeared in my mind as an unfolding vision; nothing more than an incredible act of imagination!

In that moment of revelation I realised that particles of energy are more thoughts than things; that the Universe is a mind and the key to it all was the vortex. Spin allowed the dense thought called light to appear to stand still. It gave the illusion of mass; of seemingly concrete material substance.

As I pondered on the immense realization that sprang from that cosmic picture one huge question filled my mind. Whose mind is it? Who is the dreamer, the visionary, the immense imaginer of the Universe?

My immediate answer was 'God'. I jumped to the conclusion that the Universe is the mind of God. However, Robin had warned me, "One man's truth is another man's lies. There is no absolute truth to be found. We each create our own truth as we create our own lies."

I had a problem accepting Robin's comment on truth. He was an atheist whereas I had been reared as a Roman Catholic. I believed in God as surely as he didn't.

I took Robin back to meet Pa and they struck up an immediate friendship. Pa was amazed at the maturity of the students I was mixing with and delighted that they were having a positive influence on me.

Pa told Robin he believed that there was an ultimate truth to be discovered. He had encouraged me to set out and discover it; and that is what I really wanted to do because I had an inner core of certainty that there was an ultimate truth that would unite science and religion into a single body of knowledge. Pa never doubted my conviction. I was not dismayed when others said that bridge could not be built. From my father I had learnt that people say something can't be done only because they can't conceive of it being done. Pa said to me, "If you think something can be done then just go ahead and do it."

But there were other things I did as well as think. With my brothers I learnt to sail. An elderly neighbour, Mr. Dukers was selling a clinker built sailing dingy called *Wren* for £100. Mummy Pack, who was then living with us, bought it for us with the remnant of her life savings. Wren, built before the war, had played a part evacuating soldiers off the stricken beaches of Dunkirk. She still had her original cast iron centre plate and canvas sails when we took her on. Launching her was a mission as she weighed half a ton and in the water she leaked like a sieve. We joined the Bexhill sailing club where members went out for a sail. We went out for a bail.

Not to be outdone by his sons, Pa drove to Dover in his Rolls Royce and bought an ocean going yacht for a hundred guineas. Unfortunately the *Antrona* had rot in her keel and was un-seaworthy. Pa didn't discover that until she was lifted out of the water at Rye. We never did get to sail Antrona but standing high and dry waiting to be scrapped, she became a dive for my student pals.

Simon, meanwhile, placed an order for a kit to build a state of the art racing dingy called a *Scorpion* to replace Wren. And at a club in Eastbourne he and I met two gorgeous Swedish girls.

The following year we had the Scorpion sailing and with the rising of sap came the longing to be reunited with our Swedish girlfriends. When we heard they were going to France we decided to sail across the Channel to surprise them.

It was a blue summer morning when Simon and I set out. Our compass bearing from Bexhill to Boulogne was a straight line. It looked easy sailing with a fresh breeze from the South West but there were three things we hadn't allowed for; the size of the waves in the Channel, the size of the ships in the Channel, and the plastic safety clip intended to prevent the loss of the rudder wasn't as effective as a bit of string.

Sailing along the south coast was thrilling and with the wind behind us we were making good headway until we entered the shipping lanes. Power doesn't give way to sail when power can't see the sail. Towering tankers are terrifying when viewed from a tiny twelve foot dingy trying to avoid them. Fortunately there was no fog. Out of the lanes in mid-channel we had the spinnaker up and we were spanking along when disaster struck.

I was at the helm. One hand was lightly on the tiller, the other reaching out to Simon for a sandwich when a following white horse breaking wave lifted the rudder off its pintles. I grabbed for it, I nearly leapt out of the boat after it but Simon screamed for me to stop. I stared, helpless as it floated away on the sun blinding pitiless ocean. It was gone so quickly. The rudderless craft was tossing out of control under full sail in a freshening wind. Fortunately Simon acted by reflex. He dropped the mainsail and hauled in the spinnaker lest we capsized, then handed me a paddle. It was plastic and bent as I attempted to use it to steer. I was shaking with cold and shock. Fortunately we had a wooden paddle which worked. I secured it with rope over the stern and lying in the bottom of the boat I wrestled with it to regain control of our coracle. Every wave was a battle. Every little hill of water had to be climbed and fought in the strain to maintain control. The skies were no longer blue. Menacing clouds stretched to the horizon and the south westerly had increased in force. There is no cold colder than the grey stormy sea when you are in trouble on it.

Bexhill

We heard the distant drone of an aircraft out from Lydd. Simon rummaged in a locker and pulled out the flares. It was not fear of launching air-sea rescue that stopped us; it was the deal from the chandler. He said he would give us a full refund if we returned the flares unused. They represented a lot of money for us. He must have known we might need incentive for courage. We decided to hold our course and proceed with the adventure. Simon stowed the flares as the aircraft flew almost directly overhead.

It was a hard crossing but we made it under the jib and half the mainsail right into the harbour mouth of Boulogne and then up onto the beach. Simon stowed the dingy while I went of in search of a pharmacy in a vain attempt to buy ointment to soothe my burning piles. We then had to find customs to show our passports and secure our craft. After that we phoned the family. They were glad we made it and Tim set off immediately to collect the Scorpion. He drove to Dover and manhandled the trailer onto the ferry to save the cost of taking the car. How he dragged the dingy home on the return trip was more of a mystery than how we made it safely to France. We were gone before he arrived. The longing in our loins caused us to cast aside cares as we hitched down the length of France to Cap Ferret where love awaited us; or so we hoped! Our beloved girls weren't pleased at our unexpected arrival. They'd found themselves French boyfriends to help them practice French as we had helped them practice English the summer before, so we limped home with sad hearts and me with my sore bottom. All we could do was lament our sorrows on the lyre.

Chapter 6
Light beyond light

"Music makes the soul as colour makes the flower."

Michael Ash

Simon and I took up the guitar. We'd bought a battered old instrument from Bennett's bicycle shop in St Leonards. It was hanging from a hook in the ceiling amongst rusty spoked wheels and bicycle chains. Two strings were missing and we had no idea how to tune the thing but my school chum Chris taught me a few chords and showed me how to strum. When Simon showed our musical apology to a supply teacher at college who played the guitar, she offered to teach us the rudiments of classical guitar. The first thing she did was to get us to replace our steel strung wreck with two inexpensive nylon strung classical guitars. She then showed us how to hold the instruments properly, to tune them and then she taught us two basic classical picks and several simple chord sequences. We never looked back. Within a month of her lessons I wrote my first song:

> *To the diamond of truth*
> *There are countless facets*
> *Few men can see more than one,*
> *The seeker of truth sees just one facet,*
> *And of the diamond he thinks it's the sum,*
> *Though the light of each facet is different,*
> *Each has its own tale to tell,*

In essence the light of the diamond,
Through each facet is always equal.

In that song I expressed my concern over divergent religious beliefs that were driving humanity away from spirituality and ever deeper into the morass of materialism. The only hope for the world as far as I could see was to build spiritual belief on science rather than religion.

To my way of thinking science and religion were different facets of the same diamond of truth, each revealing part but not the whole understanding of the Universe. I had been fired up with indoctrination in Roman Catholicism and then doused with the cold waters of scientific skepticism but the experiences with my father directed me to explore a middle course between the opposite extremes of religion and science. The clues I needed came from reading the two books on Yogic philosophy. Yogis described their perception of mind as a substance which they called *chitta*. With the same *siddhi* powers that they used to probe the atom to see quantum spin, they saw a fog of mind substance overlaying places where people lived. The longer people had been living in a place the denser became the mental fog.

The Indian philosophers explained that people settling in a place tended to resonate with the thoughts overlaying the place. Occasionally a powerful mind would break through with great thoughts; thoughts imbibed with love and power or empowered with genius and originality. These they perceived as flashes of lightening breaking through the dense grey clouds of the mundane and mediocre thinking of the masses.

They commented that the mental fog tended to concentrate in valleys and was less dense by the ocean. I realised from this why Pa chose to live by the sea and why my parents never settled anywhere for any length of time. Pa said there were also dangerous unseen energies in the ground where people lived so the safest thing was not to settle anywhere for more than three of four years.

I labeled the fog of thought overlaying places as the *psychosphere.* The Yogis explained that the fog of thought built up in density over generations and effected the perpetuation of established ideas and patterns of human thinking and behaviour. They also said emotions increased the density of mind substance and explained that visible light was denser still. Pa was very sensitive to these psychic energies and said the whole planet was encircled by a dense cloud of angry thoughts and emotions which made it difficult for the finer light of spirit to penetrate into our world; much as a blanket of cloud blocked out the sun.

I began to think about thought as a finer form of light. From my knowledge of science I realised thoughts could not be a higher frequency of energy than light because that would make them X-rays and gamma-rays. I knew from what Pa taught me about the link between high frequency radiation and cancer, we would all have brain tumours if we had X-rays and gamma-rays rushing round in our heads all day! Thought had to be a higher level of light in an entirely different way.

Then one day, looking out to sea it struck me that thoughts could be a form of energy beyond the speed of light; beyond our perception like land hidden beyond the horizon. Perhaps thoughts were frequencies of energy moving faster than the speed of light. Pa said to me thoughts were faster than light. The next step in my logic was to imagine the brain as a radio set transmitting and receiving the vibrations of thought. I used that to explain *telepathy* and the healing force Pa was working with. It made sense why Pa put so much store by simple radio technology. He taught me his mind affected a patient like the BBC affected a wireless. All that was required was faith. Pa believed the faith of the patient was the equivalent to tuning the patient into him. He said that is why Jesus commended in the Bible, "Your faith has made you whole.

From my reading about relativity I knew that things moving faster than the speed of light could not be contained in our space and time. Maybe there was another space and time in which thoughts move like light. That would allow a thought to leave our space and time at one point and re-enter at another. That's how I accounted for the instantaneous transmission of my father's healing thoughts across the Atlantic between England and Texas.

Then I thought about movement. Because slow speeds are part of fast speeds if the speed of thought were faster than the speed of light then our world of light would be part of the world of thought.

It struck me that if people were thinking along a certain wavelength they would 'resonate' to similar frequencies of thought in the psychosphere all around them. I realised then why angry thoughts quickly filled my head when I was upset. I was concerned at picking up other people's thoughts like germs, even though we lived by the sea where I perceived the psychosphere to be less dense we were still in a town so I wrote a prophetic poem:

A fresh wind blows in from the sea,
A wind that is free to go as it please,
It whispers a call from the wild to me,
In cities and towns people aren't free,
Tall glass buildings, prisons for men,
Factories where women are battery hens,

Even at home we're never alone,
Our thoughts aren't our own,
The air we breathe we must share,
So men and women everywhere,
Return to the green fields,
Where life can be lived without care.

The return to our own green field began with a trip to Cornwall to sort out the break down of Pa's Rolls. Tim and I had passed our driving tests but Pa only let us drive the Rolls in desperation. He had located an ex-Rolls mechanic in Cornwall and wanted Tim and I to deliver her for repairs. We were delighted to be behind the wheel of a Rolls Royce but we had problems including a dead battery and a radiator that frequently boiled. That meant we had to find a lay-by every fifty or so miles, on the top or down the slope of a hill, where we could refill with water and then roll-start the roller.

Around lunch time, steam was blowing out of the engine and I spotted a lay-by at the brow of the hill we were climbing and insisted we pull over but Tim wasn't too sure we were at the top.

"If you are wrong, you push" he said switching off the engine. I got out of the car and felt sick. We were parked just below the top of the hill. There was another fifty feet or so of 'gentle' incline. With my queer stomach I didn't feel like lunch. Tim was feeling fine so he ate my share as well as his.

When the radiator was cool enough I unscrewed the angel and refilled with water. Tim sat behind the wheel and grinned at me as I got behind to push. I heaved and strained with my back into the boot and through sheer determination I moved the heavy motor slowly forward onto the busy A30.

A queue of traffic piled up behind. As cars passed people were hanging out of their windows laughing, cheering and honking their horns at the sight of me pushing a Rolls Royce. No one offered to help. Eventually we reached the top and the strain eased as the roller began to roll over the other side. As she gained momentum down the hill, Tim selected third gear and she roared to life. I sprinted after her and leaping onto the running board I pulled open the passenger door and threw myself exhausted into the comfort of the deep, dark blue leather seat.

Meanwhile, back at home the manor of Bexhill had come on the market and Pa wanted to secure it as a centre for healing and parking suitable for his Rolls Royce. But in 700 A.D., the Saxon King Offa had given the manor of Bexhill to God for all time so despite his convictions Pa had no divine right to it. For many centuries it had been used by the church to provide for pilgrims on their way to Canterbury – St Richard of Chichester was a frequent visitor. At the Reformation the manor had passed into private hands and one of Pa's wealthy patients offered to buy it for him but the Town Council of Bexhill had other plans. They wanted to replace God's manor with a block of flats, a municipal car park and a public loo.

Pa formed an Old Town Preservation Society but there were builders on the council who were keener to develop than preserve. Using compulsory powers they purchased the manor and began the demolition. They had almost reduced it to rubble when a preservation order was slapped on some medieval walls and window mullions that were still standing. The council could neither build nor demolish. Left with a ruin to restore and preserve, they turned it into a garden; where, decades later, Àine Faylore inspired me to write this book in memorial to my father's life.

After widening the road through the old town the Council built the much-needed car park and public loo and restored the ancient tithe barn where years later Steven met his second wife Renata.

If God is nearer to us in a garden than anyone else on Earth it could be said the manor of Bexhill reverted to its rightful owner. And as for those who had cast a covetous eye on God's property, they were cast out of the garden. In a local-government re-organisation, Bexhill town council was exterminated and Pa fled from Bexhill to the field he had bought on his honeymoon, deep in the beautiful valley of Crackington Haven on the North coast of Cornwall.

The three quarter acre of trees and pasture was fabulous. Bordered by a trout stream it was connected to the outside world only by a steep narrow lane cut in the wooded hillside and a footpath to the spectacular cliffs and endless Atlantic surf just down the valley. We may have lost a manor but we regained paradise.

Ma bought a caravan and had it sited on the land over the Easter holiday of 1968. In two weeks of energy and enthusiasm we cleared brambles, set up beehives, tilled a plot and planted vegetables. We boys then returned to Bexhill to complete our college year and vacate Chantry Cottage in time for the summer holiday.

I will never forget that summer. It was the happiest time I have ever known. As a family we had nothing apart from the caravan, a hut, guitars, surfboards and Pa's convertible Bentley that had come to replace the Rolls. The days were warm and sunny and we lived out in the open, subsisting on the vegetables we had planted in the spring. Ma baked bread and milk was provided by a nanny goat called Naomi. Chickens and ducks laid eggs in abundance and Simon tickled trout from the stream.

I was the deep sea fisherman. Almost every morning, after a bath in the stream, I would don a T-shirt and a pair of jeans cut off at the knees. In place of a belt I had baler twine attached to a reel of line and some mackerel feathers. After downing porridge and toast I jogged down to the ocean, leapt onto my surfboard and paddled out to sea. Drifting on the ocean swell, sometimes just beyond the surf under the majestic cliffs, or at other times way out to sea I cast my line for mackerel, Pollock and bass.

If the surf was up I would join my brothers on their boards and ride the waves. In the late afternoon, as our valley filled with gold, we would fall, ravenous and exhausted, onto a dish of fish, fresh greens and potatoes or Jerusalem artichokes and as the sun set we gathered about an open fire to ward off the early evening chill. Then as the shadows of night drew round we picked up the guitars and played a new composition or worked out some arrangement on an old one. I caught the magic of that summer in song:

> *Listen, listen,*
> *You must just stop and listen,*
> *Listen to this song,*
> *As it weaves and flows,*
> *A little stream it tumbles,*
> *To the sea of stillness,*
> *Of peace and stillness.*

> *Listen, listen,*
> *You must just stop and listen,*
> *Listen to the music of a grasshopper's bow,*
> *Playing its song,*
> *From the world of stillness,*
> *Of peace and stillness.*

> *Listen, listen,*

Light beyond Light

You must just stop and listen,
Listen for the wind, the rustling leaves,
Whispering softly,
Of the world of stillness,
Of peace and stillness.

Listen, listen,
You must learn to stop and listen,
Listen and let life pass you on by,
For a moment just linger,
Drifting to the world of stillness,
Of peace and stillness,
Of calm stillness and peace.

Stephen captured the golden days in a haunting song:

Oh the bell tolls to the morning,
Oh the bell tolls to the sea,
Young men awake to the nets of plenty,
Following boats across the sea,

In soft flowing the breeze was sailing,
Out beyond the waters deep,
Cloud puffed skies catch seagulls wailing,
As timbers sway and canvas creaks,

Of fishes caught in times of plenty,
When cream was drawn from a cooling pail,
And bread was baked and draped with honey,
And waters drawn from a stone deep well,

Soft lowing deep in the rushes,
Waking birds rise greet the dawn,

Lifting sun drops dew in cleansing,
And fills the eyes of the nestling fawn,

Of flowers grace to weave so pretty,
Deep within dark heads of hair,
Of salty taste on lips so tasty,
Where the bell tolls of her care,

Singing songs is a croft of bracken,
Gentle Mary kneads mother's dough,
Songs to her man long hair and flowing,
Sliding through the barley sow,

Oh the bell tolls to the morning,
Oh the bell tolls to the sea,
Young men awake to the nets of plenty,
Following boats across the sea,

For a single summer we went wild. Like a family of otters we were to be found washing, playing or fishing in the stream, running barefoot through the meadows or rambling over the heather crowned hills. Every day there were Ashes in or on the ocean. We would be swimming, surfing, fishing under the cliffs, paddling out toward the horizon or simply frolicking in the shallows. The wind and the sea, the exercise and the sun made us all bronze and strong. Forsaking the world we discovered heaven and as there was no money for petrol, the Bentley stood out on the land like a presiding monument to a bygone age. And that was how Harry found us when he came down from London to visit Pa.

Chapter 7
The Vortex and the Atom

"I might not beat the establishment, but the establishment will never beat me."

Michael Ash

Despite my fascination for physics Pa wanted me to become a doctor. He argued that medicine would always provide me with an income and I could pursue physics research in my spare time as he had done. As a result of Pa's persuasive argument all but one of my applications for a place at university was for medicine and they were all turned down. During an interview at Westminster Hospital in London I was told: "We don't give medical degrees to chaps who intend to go to Australia sheep shearing as soon as they qualify!"

The only place that accepted me was Queen's University of Belfast where I had applied for a degree in Zoology. I thought I could sneak into medicine through the back door. First learn about sheep then transfer to medical school. That was possible at Queens. The first year was intermediate with a wide range of subjects giving students a better opportunity to choose the final course for their degree.

On my first afternoon in the zoology lab I was looking down a microscope. I didn't know what I was supposed to be looking for so I decided to ask for help. There were rows of students all peering down microscopes at water fleas with one or two post-graduate demonstrators dotted about the place. I spotted a fellow in a jacket, dotted with dandruff, down at the front helping someone so I strode up to him and boomed, "Excuse me please demonstrator, can you help me!"

The lab went suddenly silent. Then laughter rippled across the room. After looked up at me for a while the fellow said, "I'm not a demonstrator, I'm the professor and what are you doing in here? I don't think I've met you before!"

I flushed. I'd rocked up on the zoology course without attending an interview so I had yet to meet my professor, Gareth Owen, Head of Zoology and Dean of the Faculty of Science at Queens.

A few weeks later I made an appointment with him to discuss a transfer to medical school at the Royal Victoria Hospital. His secretary showed me his door and told me to knock and wait. I banged, expecting to hear the usual 'come in'. Instead, the door was opened and a beaming Professor Owen showed me to a chair. I was quite taken aback by the respectful way I was treated. No principal from my past had been that courteous. I had immediate respect for him.

After exchanging a laugh about our first encounter, Professor Owen spoke with passion about the way university education had become debased. He paced the room as he expressed his feelings, "Look I don't want you to take this personally," he said looking out of the window, his hands clasped tightly behind his back, "But most students come to university just to mop-up information for exams. Their only concern is to get good grades for a job. Universities are not career cram-shops or schools. At university students should be questioning what they are taught. You young people should be thinking for yourselves. Where are the impassioned debates and the new ideas? What happened to original theories and radical new world views?"

I have no idea what inspired my professor to speak to me the way he did. He could have chosen anyone. Apart from our brief encounter in the lab he had never met me before. But what he said to me that day changed my direction and propelled me back to the vortex. Transfer to medicine was never even discussed.

I left the interview determined to devote myself to developing a new worldview. From that day forward I would never concern myself about a job or attend a career interview. Instead I would develop a new theory by applying the vortex idea to physics.

I was certain in my decision. I knew I would be successful. My intuition told me it would take a lifetime but my heart was on fire at the thought of the task before me.

The idea of a vortex at the heart of matter was not new. The vortex atom had been propounded in the nineteenth century by the great Victorian scientist, Lord Kelvin who was born in Belfast. Maybe it wasn't a coincidence that I should pick up the lost thread of his theory in the city of his birth. Perhaps it was the psychosphere at work! But because Kelvin's vortex was associated with the ether it had failed to make an impact on me. As I walked the streets of Belfast in 1968, it was not Kelvin's ether vortex but the Yogic description of the atom as a vortex of energy that gripped my mind.

At the turn of the 20th Century the atom was thought to be the smallest particle of matter until in 1909 at Manchester University, Ernest Rutherford probed the atom revealing it to be mainly space with a minute nucleus. His professor at Cambridge, Sir J. J. Thomson had already discovered the electron before the turn of the 20th century and then in 1919 Rutherford went on to discover the proton.

I realised if the vortex applied to anything it had to be those subatomic particles. I determined that J. J. Thompson's electrons and Rutherford's protons were not vortices in the ether; they were vortices of energy!

After the interview I spent a lot of time in the university library reading books on physics, searching for clues to support my convictions about the subatomic vortex.

I knew that the vortex could explain the greatest mystery in physics; how energy forms mass because the whirlpool form of energy would set up a state of inertia – much as would the spin of a gyroscope.

Richard Feynman declared: *"The laws of inertia have no known origin.* I could reply "The origin of inertia is now known; it is the vortex."

I was so excited that I could account for quantum spin and I also had an easy explanation for potential energy. If particles of matter were vortices of energy obviously they would store energy!

Richard Feynman also said: *"Of nuclear energy we have the formulas for that...but not the fundamental understanding, we don't know what it is!"* I knew what it was; nuclear energy was simply the result of vortices unzipping.

I was drawn to Einstein as my father had been to Rutherford. The work of Albert Einstein became the major source of inspiration to me. His $E=mc^2$ equation of the nuclear bomb, described the release of energy stored in matter. I was convinced the atomic explosion was the unraveling of vortices of energy.

Another mystery explained by the vortex was the enigma of force fields. How could one particle of matter act on another at a distance? Electric charge, magnetism and gravity, what were they all about? Inert blobs of material could not act on each other at a distance but vortices could.

Vortices of energy were dynamic. I imagined them simply overlapping and interacting, whirling together or apart depending on their direction of spin.

I realised force fields were not things attached to particles or coming out of them; they were a natural consequence of the basic particle of matter being a vortex of energy. Electric charge was a property of the particle itself. Magnetism was an expression of its innate dynamic nature. If particles were maelstroms of energy rather than inert blobs of material then forces were a synch. As overlapping whirlpools of light, subatomic particles would obviously be acting on each other all the time.

Opposite direction of spin in the subatomic vortex - into or out of the centre - provided my account for positive and negative charge. I argued that the extending vortex energy would overlap and interact long before the particle centres come together. That was how I explained 'action at a distance'.

As energy is neither created nor destroyed I contended there would be no end to the vortex; no real boundary or surface to the particle. Like the horizon the surface of matter could be the limit of our perception of vortex energy so I determined the vortex of energy was an infinite extension. This was how I accounted for the infinite extension of electric charge, magnetism and gravity.

I had no one to share my thoughts with so I developed my ideas by imagining myself as a professor lecturing to a class of students. I reasoned to the phantom sea of enthralled faces before me that the particle of matter was just the tight centre of the vortex and that the surface of matter was where vortex energy became too thin to be perceived. I then explained to the imagined mass of enthusiastic pupils that we could not be directly aware of the sparse vortex energy beyond the surface of matter, as it would exist beyond the bounds of our perception. We could only be aware of its existence through its effects - electric charge, magnetism and gravity!

Brilliant! Genius! I could almost hear the rapturous applause. My wild imagination saw the certainty of a Nobel Prize. There was no need of a career in medicine mending mere mortals when I had mankind's understanding of the universe to mend. Ah the innocent pride of youth! I was hopelessly naïve to think I could overturn the scientific establishment and rewrite physics with a degree in zoology.

Pa taught me from when I was a mite that though he might not beat the establishment; the establishment would never beat him. I knew only what I had been taught; that an individual armed with indomitable faith in their ability to achieve can achieve anything; that nothing of real value is ever achieved in any other way!

Unconcerned at the obvious hopelessness of my task I continued to expound: "The surface of a particle is like the horizon. It does not exist in nature. It is merely the last of matter that we perceive. It is not the end of matter itself. To imagine that matter is confined to its apparent surface is the equivalent of flat earth mentality...

"The blindness of science to anything beyond direct perception is blob consciousnesses," I shouted angrily to my abstract adoring acolytes.

The idea that particles of matter are blobs of something substantial is a serious obstacle to our understanding the underlying nature of the fascinating world in which we live..." I said, sizzling in the drizzle.

"When people believe matter is formed of inert material they have to assume the existence of other things to account for the ability of particles of matter to act on each other. Forces are assumed to be something different from the particle itself."

I was not the first to walk the streets of Belfast ranting and raving of the absurdity of the material hypothesis.

"Material particles with assumed properties are a preposterous presumption." Lord Kelvin vexed in frustration as he saw the obvious account for everything in the vortex.

In my study of physics I was discovering all sorts of weird ideas and crazy speculations. Einstein imagined that matter distorted space-time. Newton assumed something was acting between bodies of matter to cause them to act on each other at a distance. When the vortex with its innate simplicity had been abandoned in favour of fashionable quantum mechanics physicists then suggested force-carrying particles popped off subatomic particles like fleas off a dog.

I could not understand why the great men of science failed to see the obvious that if mass is a form of energy, because energy is activity, particles of matter must be intrinsically active!

It was such simple, obvious logic to me. If vortex particles extend into infinity then all vortex particles must be overlapping all other particles all of the time. Therefore everything thing must be continually interacting with everything else.

"If energy is the basis of everything..." I explained to my abstract audience, "You must drop the idea of particles *with* properties. Think instead of particles *of* properties."

I explained to them that the vortex was a system of motion that behaved in a certain way. We perceived these properties of vortex motion as mass and inertia and the mysterious fields of force. Thanks to the vortex we could visualize particles as extending, overlapping constantly interacting fireballs of light rather than bounded blobs of inert material. The vortex would change forever the way we think about the world. "We humans are limited only by our fundamental assumptions and firmly held beliefs."

I had just turned twenty. Confident I had cracked the code of creation I decided to share my ideas about the subatomic vortex with one of the physics lecturers. So far I had kept my ideas to myself and confided in no one. The time had come for me to share my revolutionary vortex physics with a professional physicist. I apprehended one tidying up plastic sheets on the overhead projector after a lecture. I asked if he had time to hear a new theory. In a thick Ulster accent he said yes so long as it didn't take too long. He then stopped what he was doing and listened intently to what I had to say.

I drew spirals and I spoke very quickly but he grasped my ideas. When I finished he said, "I am impressed with what you have done but I can see flaws in your argument. I can't see, according to your vortex theory, how particles can exist without charge so how do you explain the neutron?"

I was elated by his commendation. The neutron was easy to explain; or so I thought!

"The electron and proton vortices would be attracted together by opposite directions of spin," I expounded cupping my hands into each other to demonstrate the affect of the force of charge.

"As they converge the charge effect of each vortex would be cancelled out by the presence of the other; as occurs in the atom," I continued enthusiastically, "Atoms are electrically neutral because they have an equal number of opposite charges so the neutron would be neutral because it contains a pair of opposite charges which cancel each other out."

"Neutrality in the atom comes from the co-existence of opposite charges. However the same can not be said of the neutron because the neutron is not an electron bound to a proton," he replied.

"Why not," I argued, "A neutron can be formed out a proton and electron. The mass of a neutron is that of an electron and proton. In a matter of minutes neutrons out of the atom fall apart into protons and electrons. It is obvious a neutron is an electron bound to a proton."

The lecturer squared his shoulders and looked up at me intently. "I am sorry," he said emphatically, "It is clear from quantum theory that the neutron can not be a bound state of electron and proton!"

I was deflated and mystified. This was the first of many times physicists would reject my proposal for the neutron without giving me reason. Years were to pass before I would realise I had struck a fundamental flaw in quantum theory. I didn't know it at the time but in my innocence I had uncovered something scientists were trying to hide. At the time I had no idea my discovery would lead to an exocet that could vindicate my father and blast the scientific establishment to kingdom come. That would come later!

As he packed the last of his papers in his brown leather briefcase he looked at me again and said, "A vortex spins on an axis, it has poles and is conical in shape but subatomic particles are spheres without poles. How do you explain that?"

I had no explanation. I said I would work on the problem of poles. He said I should report back to him with the solution, if I could find one.

I thanked him for his time and slunk away.

Gripped by the twisted guts of defeat my usual hearty appetite for lunch vanished. The vortex theory appeared to be vanquished. My brain-baby lay writhing in mortal agony at my feet. I could see no resolution to the dilemma of the poles. How could a vortex exist without an axis of spin? Career interviews flashed before my fate. I would have to get a job. The appalling prospect of a normal life without a Nobel Prize left me in a state of devastating desperation. How could a vortex exist without poles? The shining gold of glory crumbled into dreary dust as my mind tormented me with the folly of thinking I had the answer to everything when I couldn't find an answer to the very first question I was asked. I abandoned my vortex theory and plunged into the fleshpots of student life.

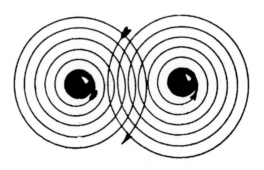

Vortex fields of force

Chapter 8
The Ball of Wool

"If you want to discover the truth you must do it for the love of science not the love of money."

Michael Ash

In an attempt to take my mind off the vortex I sat in on geology lectures where I learnt why Pa found uranium in Cornwall and why it was no coincidence our original road dig was close to an ancient copper mine. There were plenty of other things to distract me. The Belfast Festival was in full swing so I indulged in jazz and folk music along with numerous classical concerts but they failed to lift my depression. My confidence in the mystics of India was shattered. If yogic insight into the atom didn't fit with science how could I trust their other observations? I was in a crisis of faith. How could my deep sense of knowing I was right be so wrong? Only the traditional Irish music with the penny whistle, drum and pipes broke through my cloud of despair. The haunting Gaelic sound brought me in touch with a spirit that could remain merry in the face of all adversity.

In the Mourne Mountains, I mourned the loss of my universal understanding in a melancholy song:

> *Rove, rove, rove, rover, a rover is my heart,*
> *Searching for some boundless sea*
> *A thousand leagues afar,*
> *Although it search it never finds,*

Seek hard though it may,
For that sea's far, far away.

Though we're young and careless,
We're neither bound nor free,
For deep down we're all searching,
For that we never see,
Although we're led there's none that lead,
If we ask we're told,
To look out for a flower never of seed.

Some they search for money,
Some for another's arms,
Some they search for nothing,
Oh they died before they were born,
But money's lost whenever it's found,
And another's arms are frail,
The rock we reach for turns out to be nothing but shale.

Our fathers they were hungry,
They lived from day to day,
But now we're fed we hunger,
For their faith that never swayed,
A hungry man has his dreams,
His hopes for a better day,
But a man with wealth has nothing for which to pray.

Rove, rove, rove, rover, a rover is my heart,
Searching for some boundless sea
A thousand leagues afar,
Although it search it never finds,
Seek hard though it may,
For that sea's far, far away,

The onset of a bleak winter and the brooding dissatisfaction in Northern Ireland didn't help. The mood was oppressive. I hated the thought of disappointing Professor Owen and the outlook of life without discovery was desolate. Belfast in '68, was beginning to breed bleak outlooks. It certainly bled my heart. The student society at Queens was merry enough. Alcohol sloshing in student skins brightened the gloom but not mine. Apart from an occasional half pint of Guinness and a thoughtful pipe of *Three Nuns* I was a sober and solitary figure, plodding and shivering on the grey, sleet flecked streets, haunted by the ghost of the vortex.

I knew intuitively that the Yogi's were right about matter being spin but my mind continued to torment me with doubts. There had to be an answer to the axis problem but I couldn't resolve it no matter how hard I tried. I wrestled the conundrum alone as my class of imagined followers had evaporated. The remaining weeks of term dragged by remorselessly. I longed for Christmas.

Despite the wild weather and mud that greeted me on my return to Cornwall, it was a joy to be back home on the land. Our green acre was heaven compared to Belfast and the Haven nursed my troubled spirit. Sitting by the swollen stream as it tumbled toward the sea I found solace in the damp softness of Cornwall. Weeping woodlands matched my sadness. Tears of damp dripping from forlorn branches reminded me of the careless days of golden summer gone and a brief glorious autumn lost forever. Blue days of fishing and bright dreams of fame and fortune faded. The wild winter ocean would not tolerate my flimsy line of feathers any more than the rigours of science my slim line of reasoning, but the ceaseless rolling ocean soothed my soul nonetheless.

I knew in my heart the subatomic vortex was the key to the universe but the swirling seas brought me no closer to resolving the secret that eluded my mind. I slithered over seaweed rocks and stared into the limpet pools in hope of resolving the greatest mystery in physics but to no avail. When my brothers joined me at the shore I abandoned metaphysics for madness. Leaping into the icy ocean with nothing but a torn wetsuit and a battered surfboard I allowed the frantic rollers thrown ashore by Atlantic winter storms to beat my brains senseless.

Pa's Bentley was no longer to be found sheltering behind the caravan on the land. Harry's arrival had changed everything. Harry was inspired by our ideals. Realising we had recovered something the world had lost he decided to join the family. Plunging a couple of thousand pounds into Pa's commune he had moved from London onto the land.

But Pa didn't hang out in the mud with Harry. He had enjoyed living off the land in the summer but Ma was a practical woman. She knew Cornwall only too well. Winter was no time to linger with ideals. The caravan had no electric and the only running water was rain.

Tim was desperately ill from the condition he contracted at birth. A revolutionary liver bypass had saved his life but not his health. The windswept valley in winter was no place for a chronic invalid. Ma also needed a home near the road where Mary and Richard could catch the school bus. Harry's contribution was a Godsend providing rent for a winter cottage in Higher Crackington.

Pa was easily persuaded from his principles. He was happy to exchange the damp cold caravan and morning dips in the bone chilling stream for warm cottage comforts and steaming hot baths. His ideals for the simple life were not rooted in nobility; they were forced on him. He only lived on the land because he was broke and had nowhere else to live.

So it was that Harry, safely separated from his savings, found himself marooned in the caravan. The only members of the commune left for his company were Sir Lancelot the sheep dog, Naomi the nanny goat and Pia the Devon red calf along with Charlie the cockerel and his harem of hens and twenty ducks Tim had reared through the summer.

On milder autumnal days Tim occasionally strolled down into the valley to tend the stock and chat. At weekends Pa would arrive in the baronial Bentley with Richard and lots of enthusiastic suggestions for land practice which Harry was expected to put into operation. However, when winter gales and horizontal rain came howling up the valley, Tim's visits became less frequent and Pa's none at all. Only Sir Lancelot remained loyal.

As much as he loved the dog Harry loathed the goat. Naomi was a reincarnate fiend sent to torment him. She continually broke into the vegetable patch despite his best endeavours to secure the fence. If he hobbled her, like Houdini she would slip her knots and head for his spring greens. Harry could swear she laughed at him as she gaily dodged the clods he hurled at her. He told me of a nightmare he had of being chased by galloping hordes of Genghis Khan. He woke in a sweat to discover it was the sound of Naomi trotting on and off the deck outside the caravan. In a fury he opened the door and threw the nearest thing to hand; the torch. He missed. Demented, he donned his dressing gown and plunged out into the rain-drenched, wind-tossed darkness. As he pulled on a gumboot his foot sank into softness. Shocked at the tween-toe squelch of goat dung, he slipped off the sodden deck and fell headfirst into the mud.

We loved Naomi. She had provided us with two pints of milk a day throughout the summer. Apart from occasionally kicking over the bucket when it was full, none of us had any complaint against her. But then, in temperament, she was closer to the Ashes than to Harry.

Harry rated his companions according to their intelligence. Sir Lancelot, a farm dog of uncertain breed with an insatiable desire to herd, was smartest. Naomi was next with that wicked craftiness typical of the diabolical. Pia wasn't bright but what she lacked in brains she made up in brawn. Charlie wasn't clever but he was a gentleman. When he found a worm he would toss it aside so that one of his hens could snatch it up. As the ducks had lost their heads when they disappeared into an unscrupulous duck rustler's deep freeze they had no place on Harry's scale of intelligence.

Harry did his best to keep the stock on the land but it was a hapless task. Pia followed Naomi everywhere and their favourite destination was Reading's cottage garden. The Readings were an elderly couple who lived in quiet retirement on the other side of the valley. Naomi shared Mr. Reading's passion for roses, but it wasn't the sight of the goat leaping his gate to browse his flower beds that really distressed Mr. Reading; it was the calf. Thinking she was a goat but unable to leap like a goat, Pia would crash right through the gate. The half grown Devon Red appeared on his plot like the Panzers on Poland. The delicate tread of the goat left no trace but the calf demolished the patch and left steaming pats of Reading's reconstituted herbaceous borders on the path.

In response to raging Reading, Harry attempted to tether the troublesome two. Most goats would happily munch their way through the day at the end of a rope but not Naomi, somehow or other she always broke loose and managed to free the calf as well. Honest to God, I caught sight of Naomi on top of a pile of building blocks undoing a knot in the rope around Pia's neck with her teeth!

It was the promise of our return to the caravan that kept Harry on until Christmas. He was genuinely looking forward to our company. Pa had convinced him that when we arrived home from college all we would want to do was till the sod and tend the stock but unaware of Harry's expectations we arrived wishing only to catch waves and play guitars. We had no intention of working the land.

After an hour or two in the winter surf we were too numb and exhausted to handle a hoe. It was early evening before we recovered from our ordeal in the freezing water and by then it was too dark to toil. Most evenings Harry would cook supper. We would do the dishes and then play on our guitars, sometimes until the early hours of the morning. We slept until noon then jogged down to the Haven to wander on the rocks or take a hammering in the thundering surf.

Harry was utterly disillusioned but still confessed we were better company than the goat! Fortunately he had a sense of humour and admitted to enjoying our music. He introduced me to theosophy, Gnosticism and the teaching of Gurdjieff but it was not for his metaphysics he was heaven sent. Harry led me out of the impasse I had reached with the vortex.

The breakthrough came one evening after supper. Stephen and Simon were strumming on their guitars and I was drying the dishes. When I finished Harry asked if I would hold up a hank of wool for him so he could wind it into a ball.

As I sat watching Harry winding his ball of wool the problem of the axis of spin resolved before my unblinking eyes. He was winding the wool in a three dimensional spiral in which the axis of spin was continually changing. Harry was forming a vortex; but it was a ball. I stared at the *spherical vortex* transfixed. I was mesmerised by Harry's vortex. It had no single axis of spin. As Harry wound the wool onto the ball I could see energy spinning to form the characteristic corpuscular particles of matter.

To begin with I was stunned then I was ecstatic. At last I had a viable model for the subatomic particle. The ball of wool was a spherical vortex with axes that could not be measured because they constantly moving. It had poles that could not be discerned because they were changing all the time! As Harry continued to wind the ball, it grew larger and I imagined if I looked at it in cross section, it would appear like concentric spheres. These would grow or shrink depending on whether wool was wound on or off the ball. That was how I came to picture the subatomic particle both as a spherical vortex and a system of expanding or contracting concentric spheres.

In those memorable moments of winding wool, earth-shattering realisations rushed into my mind. I could see why the vortex of energy didn't have the traditional shape of a cone. A ball of wool is not a cone because the wool is free to be wound in every direction. It winds in a ball because that is the only way it can wind when it has total freedom in its spin. In the subatomic vortex of energy - the *'quantum vortex'* as I now prefer to call it – there is nothing to keep energy spinning in any one plane. It is free to spin in a different plane from one instant to the next and it does just that. Because of its freedom to spin on infinite axes the vortex of energy is a perfect sphere without measurable poles.

When I returned to Belfast after Christmas I wasted no time in breaking the news. The lecturer was impressed,

"You should consider joining our department," he said, "We could do with a mind like yours."

"I will think about it," I replied but fear again gripped my stomach. To do physics I would have to study mathematics and that was a no, no for me.

As a six year old at prep school in Bude I received the ruler across my knuckles at the end of every math lesson for adding my multiplication sums. I had refused to memorise my multiplication tables. I wasn't a parrot! So I was threatened with the cane if I persisted. Fortunately the very day they were going to deliver the blows to my bottom my parents took me out of the school. I cannot describe the sense of relief as I peered out of the rear window of the car that drove me away from that school for the last time. Nonetheless the damage was done. Associating mathematics with pain, I was deterred from numeracy forever.

Perhaps it was intended I be deterring from mathematics as arithmetical calculations would have taken me into the realms of *how* rather than *why*. Caught up in algebra I could have lost my impetus for originality. Equations would have deterred me from analogies and pictures. Mathematics would have led me from simplicity to complexity and blocked my ability to communicate my work to everyone rather than just a few scientists.

I believe there is an over emphasis on mathematics in physics. My views are shared by Gary Zukav. Many years later I read in his 'The Dancing Wu Li Masters': *The fact is that physics is not mathematics...Stripped of mathematics, physics becomes pure enchantment.*

To do a degree in physics was also out of keeping with my calling. It would betray the direction of my father and Professor Owen. My professor had voiced concern at the loss of the amateur pioneering scientist and original thinker.

He had expressed alarm at the ever-narrowing fields of specialization encouraged by the school, college and university system. His plea to me was to be a courageous mind and think outside of the confines set up by disciplines of study. To study physics formally would have been a betrayal to his ideals so I decided to continue to read physics alone and unaided. I chose to develop my life work as a passion not as a profession. It was to be a hobby, not a career. Like Dr Oliver Sacks who graduated in medicine yet maintained his passion for chemistry throughout his life, I wanted to keep the flame of the amateur-pioneering scientist alive as my father had done before me. Despite my dream of a Nobel Prize, my motivation in physics would remain a passionate love of the subject, not the lure of money or fame. That was the difference between the amateur and the professional.

Though I was at university I chose to live and work in an intellectual vacuum. A mental greenhouse was necessary to protect the vortex physics in the early formative years and I depended on serendipity. Harry and his ball of wool was an outstanding example of that.

I knew my work was for a new age; an age when everyone would be enlightened with a complete understanding of the universe. I expressed this ideal in song:

A new day is dawning,
In floods the tide,
Just watch where you're standing
Or you may be swept aside,
The ground on which we stand,
Is falling from our feet,
Spread your wings and fly,
Or stay to die.

The Ball of Wool

A new day is dawning,
It has long been prophesied,
The old world is passing,
A new one will rise,
An autumn leaf is falling,
It leaves a bud behind,
After winter's night,
This will burst into new life.

A new day is dawning,
Come love take my hand,
Together we will stride,
Toward tomorrow's beckoning land,
This day is now in turmoil,
It will fall we will stand,
Love bring fresh your mind,
Leave all else behind.

A new day is dawning,
In man's spirit, in his mind,
His land will still need tilling,
To a home she'll be confined,
And four winds will go on blowing
With the flood and ebb of tide,
But the new day will bring,
True peace within.

Back in Belfast, walking under the willows by the river Lagan, I pondered alone on the structure of the Universe. I thought about Einstein and his early years. He was an amateur pioneer. I admired his courage. Sometimes I felt he was with me as I walked with my lonely thoughts.

In the 20th century of Einstein everyone thought of energy purely in the form of waves. I realised they had only half the picture. The vortex was a form of energy overlooked. The great Victorian scientist, Lord Kelvin, had walked the same streets that I walked, watched the same river Lagan flow by and thought the same thought. He knew the waveform of energy gave rise to heat and light but he reckoned the vortex was responsible for the smallest particles of matter and the forces associated with them. But I wasn't destined to remain in Belfast with my resurrection of Kelvin's vortex theory for matter. We woke up one morning with no water in Belfast. The IRA had blown up the aqueducts from the Mourne Mountains. The storm had broken.

The ball of wool spherical vortex discovered in the caravan on our land

Chapter 9
Careering into Nutrition

"Without cranks engines won't run."

Michael Ash

When the British Army moved into Belfast in 1969 I moved out. Pa had insisted I wasn't to return. He suggested I transfer to a university in England and contacted Professor Owen who replied to say that there was no precedent for transfer from one university to another but, considering the extenuating circumstances, he would see what he could do. He was on his way to a conference at Queen Elizabeth College of London University. He said that while he was there he would put in a transfer request for me. He was as good as his word and arranged for my relocation. The college didn't offer a course in zoology but a corner was found for me in the department of biochemistry and physiology.

It was early October 1969 when I packed my bag and set off with my guitar for London. I decided to catch a coach to Exeter, as hitching out of North Cornwall was difficult. On the coach, bored at staring out on the endless fields of cows and sheep, I cast a casual glance at the prospectus for Queen Elizabeth College. What I read galvanized me. Queen Elizabeth College had a faculty of nutrition founded by John Yudkin who first warned of the danger of sugar. My dormant passion for nutrition was immediately rekindled.

In 1968 I had written and duplicated a paper on whole food nutrition. I was certain degenerative disease was a consequence of malnutrition in modern society, and good nutrition was the medicine of the future. I could not stay in my seat. I paced the aisle, contemplating the possibility of doing a degree in nutrition. There was no doubt in my mind. I would embark on that course immediately.

The following day I had an interview with someone in biochemistry. Before he had time to open his mouth I said "Please, rather than waste your time, can you arrange for me to see someone in the nutrition department."

He got on the phone immediately and five minutes later I was in the office of Dr. Bender, John Yudkin's assistant. There happened to be one place left on the first year course, which started the very next day. He accepted me on the spot. My career as a nutritionist settled, all I needed was a place to stay.

I strolled across to the main entrance of the college and scanned the notice board. There was a postcard advertising lodgings for a music student. That was for me. Grabbing my bag and guitar I headed off to Campden Hill Square, Kensington. The elegant terraced house was within easy walking distance of the college and Holland Park - to my mind the best park in London. I knocked on the door and was welcomed in by a well-spoken New Zealander who introduced herself to me as Mrs. Weir.

"Actually I am looking for a music student," she said, "I have a baby grand piano and I want someone who can practice on it. Can you play?"

"I can't play the piano but I do play the guitar!" I replied enthusiastically.

"I would prefer someone who could play the piano but since you are the only person to reply to my advertisement maybe I should consider you?

It is hardly surprising no one answered the advertisement because there were no music students at Queen Elizabeth College!

"Let me play you one of my songs then you can decide."

"Come on in then," she opened the door wide, "I charge five pounds a week for bed, breakfast and evening meal but you have to provide for yourself at lunch and wash your own clothes."

The front room had that costly cosiness characteristic of plush London homes. I took an immediate liking to the place, and to Mrs. Weir.

I took out my guitar and sang a couple of songs. Mrs. Weir was enchanted and offered me the room. Now I had both a comfortable home and a surrogate mum. I paid her twenty pounds for a month in advance and moved in.

Initially, I set out with the intention of devoting myself to the study of nutrition. However, an unseen hand kept nudging me back to physics. To begin with I resisted.

"Why me," I protested to a tree in the park, "How can I take on the world of physics? I am mathematically incompetent and physics is such a daunting subject. Nutrition is more my subject..."

I was tremendously excited about the opportunity of reading nutrition as a degree. I remembered all the work I had done, making my own mineral supplements and supporting my father in his vitamin solution to alcohol. Through my dad I had a vitamin pedigree.

For a few weeks of weakness I was on course for a career in nutrition but as always, whenever I attempted to put the physics aside sooner or later some chance circumstance would impel me back to it; a conversation with someone, or a book I picked up, a newspaper article or a television programme that I just happened to watch. I rarely did proper research. The information I needed usually fell into my lap. Knowledge had to drop out of the sky and hit me on the head; only then would I take notice. Those who knew me saw a mix of craziness and laziness. But this combination turned out to be perfect. It protected me from unnecessary information. I was sailing into uncharted waters. I had little idea of what I needed to know from one moment to the next. I couldn't navigate in the waters of physics so I relaxed and allowed myself to be blown at random by the winds of serendipity.

I had ample faith. My father, though Catholic, retained the wisdom and indomitable faith of his Jewish ancestry. He schooled me to trust that whatever I needed would always come to me. So it happened. I needed a textbook on nutrition for my course work. It was a massive tome, far beyond my slender means so I went searching among the second hand textbooks on sale in the student union. I rummaged through the boxes but there was nothing on nutrition. However, I spotted a dog-eared textbook titled, 'Modern University Physics'.

I kept putting the book back then picked it up again. I couldn't resist it so I bought it for a couple of shillings. Immediately I turned to the last page and read: *With the exception of continued work on the process of fusion, physicists have turned away from devising nuclear reactors, and are back at the task of unraveling the basic problems of the structure of matter. The newest particles found in high-energy processes are completely foreign to our present scheme of things. Let us hope that out of this chaotic riddle will come a profound and simplifying answer. We may be likened to those who knew only Ptolemy's complex description of the solar system. What we need is a Copernicus to assimilate and interpret the data with a generalization, which will not only solve the riddle, but lift our sights to levels we cannot now foresee.*

From that concluding statement I knew the book was for me. Though I had resisted there was now a certainty in me that I had to get back to work on the physics.

I loved that book. It was my constant companion for years and gave me the basic information I needed for the next phase of development of the vortex physics.

The thing that excited me most in 'Modern University Physics' was a revolutionary experiment that really showed me the value of the vortex.

It told the story of how in 1932, Carl Anderson of the California Institute of Technology discovered the very first bit of *antimatter* anyone had ever seen. An extremely high energy photon of light had somehow been transformed into matter and antimatter as it passed through the nucleus of a heavy atom. The antimatter didn't last long. As soon as it met matter, the two particles annihilated and the gamma ray energy appeared again.

I found the discovery of antimatter incredibly easy to explain with the vortex. As the two lines of the movement of light in the photon flew into the vortex particles in the nucleus of the atom, they were forced into vortex motion. Two new vortex-particles then appeared on the other side of the atomic nucleus. One was matter and the other antimatter because their vortex spin was opposite. When the two opposite vortices spun together they 'unzipped' one another. The two equal but opposite whirlpools of light had cancelled each other out. The energy released then radiated away as wave trains of light. Waves turned to vortices then turned back into waves; simple as a pimple!

I explained this to my imagined class of students, who had recently reappeared in my mind, by analogy with pasta. The vortices in the nuclei of the lead atoms were like pasta formers. When pasta squeezes through a 'pasta former' it takes on the pasta shape. When energy is forced through the vortices in an atomic nucleus it takes on the shape of the vortex. Thus energy is transformed into mass.

I reasoned that just as wool does not cease to exist when it is knitted from a compact ball into the spread of a wooly jumper, so the energy in the vortices of antimatter and matter did not vanish when annihilated; they were merely transformed from static particles of matter into propagating wave-particles of light.

Explaining antimatter gave me confidence to write my first paper. We didn't have computers and printers in those days, not even photocopiers! All I had was a mechanical typewriter and an antiquated Roneo Duplicator the Neives of Enfield had left Pa when they passed away. I typed out my ideas onto stencils. Then I etched line drawings onto them. These were then loaded onto the drum of the duplicator, which was then turned by hand. It picked up ink from a roller where the letters and lines were on the stencil and transferred these onto rough paper – it had to be coarse to absorb the ink which led to a very rough presentation.

Unfortunately I had no success in getting my paper published in a scientific journal. Being an undergraduate nutritionist didn't help my cause to rewrite fundamental physics. My father sent a copy of my paper for review to Sir Martin Ryle, the Astronomer Royal who had been one of his playmates as a boy. Ryle's reply was the first of many rebuffs I was to receive. Sir Martin said there was nothing in my work that was not adequately explained by quantum mechanics and my paper reminded him of medieval philosophers attempting to work out how many angels could stand on the head of a pin. He added a further crushing remark, I would be better to stick to my studies in nutrition and leave physics to the professionals!

Pa put an understanding hand on my shoulder, "When we were boys I gave him a piggy back ride and bucked him on his head. I think he's just getting his own back!"

A glancing thought passed through my head. One day I would buck quantum mechanics on its head! Undeterred by Ryle's derogatory comments I decided to ask the professor of mathematics at my college to read the paper. When I went back to see him and he realised I was not a student in his department, he was angry.

"You have an audacity to think you can come up with original ideas in physics when you are not even studying the subject!" he exclaimed angrily. "I strongly recommend you drop this nonsense theory of yours and get back to your studies in nutrition and in future keep your nose in your degree subject and out of affairs that are of no concern of yours!"

I was disappointed but not defeated. Professor Owen replied to my paper encouraging me to continue. Although he couldn't comment on the content because it was out of his field, he felt what I was doing was important and I should persist. Persist I did. Despite setbacks I never give up on the vortex. Like my dad I was a crusader for amateur science and unraveling mysteries in physics was a joy to me. With each breakthrough I was lifted to the heady heights of ecstasy, the rare preserve of pioneers in science on the lonely journey of discovery.

Before I moved to London we made another discovery; we had dug the septic tank in the wrong place! It happened on Easter Sunday, 1969.

We'd been granted planning permission to build a dwelling on the land because Pa had drawn up plans before the planning act came into force. A local builder called Mike Preller had designed a magnificent house and the patient who'd offered to buy the manor lent Pa £5,000 toward the construction. Everything was set to go but Ma was impatient. It was Easter Sunday and she didn't want an Easter egg, she wanted a new home. She was in a mood before we went to church and when we got back she blew her stack. She shouted through her tears that we were a load of lazy louts and refused cooked breakfast unless we got started on the construction. We tried to explain to her that we had to wait for the builders and we didn't know what to do or where to start but to no avail. Ma just screamed louder. Then Pa had a brainwave. "We'll get started on the septic tank right now!" he shouted and hollered at us to get the picks and shovels.

We were livid. The surf was brilliant, our mates were gathering at the Haven and girl friends were expected in the afternoon. The last thing we wanted to do was dig a sh*t hole. But arguing with Ma and Pa made them only angrier so swearing and cursing we hit the dig. Pa chose an obvious looking spot and we attacked the ground with fury. Apart from missing the surf, the beach buddies and the girls along with Steven bashing his head with a pick when it bounced off a rock and Pa and Richard getting in everyone's way, we applied ourselves to the task and by late afternoon the pit was dug and Ma was happy.

Mike Preller heard rumours of events up the valley and strolled in on Tuesday morning to see what we were up to. "You should have spoken to me first," he remarked with a broad grin, "The hole you dug is too close to the house site for a septic tank."

Pa started to argue with him but Mike just replied, "Argue with the building inspector. You'll have to dig another hole ten meters further out to satisfy him."

Then Pa had a brainwave. "I know," he declared bright eyed with enthusiasm, "We can turn the hole into a fugu."

A fugu is an ancient Cornish shelter consisting of a hole in the ground covered in branches and bracken. Only Richard and Mike were delighted at Pa's innovation; Richard because he was as keen to build a Hobbit hole as Pa and Mike because of the entertainment value in our reaction to Pa's suggestion. But Mike's humour was masked by a serious concern. The money Pa had raised was only half his estimate for building the house. A week after Easter Mike resolved the dilemma in a single stroke of inspired genius; or so he thought! Pa had just received a letter from an American entrepreneur expressing an interest in his alcohol antidote and was discussing it with me when Mike walked into our conversation and dropped the suggestion that we ask for a £5,000 non-refundable deposit before entering into any negotiations. Pa thought the idea was brilliant and got me to write a letter immediately. By the time I arrived back in Cornwall for the summer vacation Pa had banked the cheque but he had no intention of spending the money on the house. He and Ma were already blowing it on an extravagance in London and a family holiday. Ma had bought a small towing caravan and an uncomfortable Land Rover to tow it with leaving just sufficient money for the trip. None of us argued, it sounded like fun and for some reason our parents were emphatic about the importance of a family holiday.

We set out on a warm summer day for the Southampton to Cherbourg ferry. Simon was at the wheel. As we approached Salisbury we were hot and thirsty and as it was a little after three Ma suggested we stop for tea. There were lots of delightful teashops in Salisbury. Simon negotiated the narrow streets while Ma looked out for signs advertising tea and scones. Suddenly Pa announced he knew a place where we could get tea for free. Deaf to Ma's apprehensions frugal Simon followed Pa's directions. As he pulled into the Cathedral Close, Ma's misgivings mounted by several decibels. By the time Pa followed by Tim, David, Simon, Steven, Mary, Peter and Richard were scrunching on the gravel in a steady stride toward the Bishop's Palace, Ma was screaming, "Michael, Michael..." but to no avail; Pa was selectively deaf to his wife's high frequency howls.

After a heavy beating the palace door gave way to a bewildered, bespectacled bishop who invited us all in. Desperately trying to remember how he had come by these delightful though unexpected visitors, Pa jogged his memory. Fifteen years earlier when they met at a healing conference the Bishop had suggested, "If ever you're passing through Salisbury do drop by!"

Too polite and charitable to turn us away he suggested we stop for tea. Our timing was impeccable. The drawing room was already set with fine bone china and piles of fresh cucumber sandwiches. As Pa engaged the bishop in theology, two teenagers graced by the holy loins ran back and forth with cream scones and Victoria sponges. We scoffed. Sipping a second cup of tea with some satisfaction, I looked out over the legendary Constable landscape from the deep cushions of a bishopric couch. Tim leaned across and whispered, "I think Pa found the best place for tea in Salisbury."

As we left the palace we passed the church commissioners coming up the path. All we left them were dry biscuits for tea.

Apart from driving out of a Breton village without Peter and Ma and Mary climbing onto urinals in a campsite toilet mistaking them for bidets we enjoyed a fairly normal holiday. The one infuriation was a sack of sea salt Pa threw in the back of the Land Rover that obstructed our feet all the way home. We wanted to throw it out onto the road but Pa wouldn't let us. However when it came to annual accounts the entire cost of the trip including the caravan and Land Rover was written off against tax as a research expedition. Pa argued he had sourced a supply of trace elements for mineralised sugar so the tax man didn't get any of the American money but neither did Mike Preller. St Mark was watching over us but not poor Preller. He should have known that his only hope to obtain the cost of building the house for us at Congdons Bridge was to locate the patron saint for builders then drop to his knees and pray.

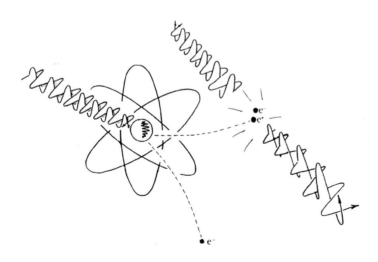

The drawing I did at Congdons of the creation & annihilation of antimatter

Congdons Bridge

Chapter 10
Bubbles of Space

"Breakthroughs often come without looking for them."

Michael Ash

One late afternoon I was in the library of Queen Elisabeth College, overlooking Campden Hill road. I had been struggling with notes my friend Elaine had copied for me from a physiology lecture. Whenever I skipped a lecture to follow my own research I would give another student carbon paper to slip between the pages of a notepad so I had duplicate notes to revise from. Thus I managed to keep abreast with my course work.

That afternoon I couldn't concentrate on the scrawl of hurried handwriting I was endeavouring to decipher. I felt an irresistible urge to get up and visit the physics shelves of the library. I lifted myself up but then sat down, determined to persist with my degree studies. After a minute or two I was up again. I couldn't settle. The urge to browse the physics shelves of the library was irresistible.

With truant guilt I walked across the room. As I did so a glow filled me. When I browsed amongst the books it grew stronger then turned to excitement as my eye alighted on a small, green hardback. I snatched it from the shelf and opened it at random.

Words leapt out of the pages. They described a principle Einstein had worked out in one of his thought experiments, which he called the *Principle of Equivalence of Forces*. He used the analogy of a box dropping from a high altitude. A man inside the falling box would have no way of knowing that he was being pulled by gravity toward his doom. During the drop he would be floating, weightless because the acceleration of his box toward Earth would have cancelled out the effect of gravity.

Einstein then imagined the box in a rocket. Even in outer space, millions of miles from the gravity of Earth, the man would fall toward the back of the box as it accelerated forward. The acceleration mimicked the force of gravity.

Einstein reasoned that the man in the box would have no way of knowing if gravity were due to a force field, or acceleration. In the principle, Einstein declared that it would be impossible to prove by experiment whether a force were due to either the action of a force field or acceleration. The book went on to explain how he developed the general theory of relativity from this idea.

I left the library for the loo wondering why the information was important for me. I often had insights during a pee and on this occasion the image of fast winding spools on a tape recorder popped into my mind. I recalled how the spinning tape caused the spools to accelerate. The reel-to-reel tape recorders used to record our songs demonstrated how motion in a spiral caused acceleration toward its centre. Returning to the library I thought about the spinning spools. A spherical vortex sliced in half would appear something like a spiral of tape on a tape-recorder.

I went back to the little green book and did a thought experiment. First I imagined that I was small enough to sit inside a subatomic vortex. Looking out along a radius at another vortex of energy I realised that it would appear as something accelerating toward me or away from me.

I then shifted my mental point of view. Now I was looking down on the vortices from above. From this perspective they appeared as two force fields of swirling energy overlapping and interacting.

Standing at the library bookshelf I realised if Einstein's principle for gravity could be applied to the vortex account for charge I had a way of unifying gravity and electro-magnetism. I looked down at the book again, my heart beating with excitement. Was the vortex of energy the unified field that Einstein was searching for? As I thought I realised I could also reconcile Newton and Einstein. My mind was buzzing with excitement. I still recall the glow of the air in the room. Standing with that little green book in my hand I saw the contradictory theories of Newton and Einstein merge into a single vortex account for force.

What I saw in that vivid moment was that the two men were merely taking different points of view. Newton was taking the point of view of two bodies moving due to a force operating across space. Einstein was taking the point of view two bodies moving relative to each other without reference to an external void of space.

As I stood at the bookshelf, the light outside was fading and rain pattered on panes nearby. Deep in thought I walked across to the window and watched the cars in the shining street of Campden Hill below.

I imagined myself as Sir Isaac Newton looking down on the scene. Newton frequently retired to Kensington to escape the bustle of London and stress of running the Royal Mint. It was a sleepy village in his day. He would have walked up that same Campden Hill and perhaps strolled over the meadows down from Notting Hill Gate and through the woods now in Holland Park. He would have walked along muddy, winding, tree-lined lanes where today there are city streets. Watching horse drawn carts and carriages move up and down Campden hill, as I was watching cars, it is unlikely Newton would have questioned the nature of the space they moved through. To him space was the emptiness above the road through which things moved. It was the void placed by God, occupied by heavenly bodies and men, that all might traverse their way.

I was looking down on Newton's country in a different era. I had a book on Einstein's general theory of relativity in my hand. Einstein thought about space in a very different way. As a five year old his father had given him a compass to play with when he was ill in bed. As he moved the compass about he was fascinated by the way the needle remained in the same place. This led his boyish mind to conclude that space was holding the needle. From then on he thought of space not as absolute nothingness, but as something real.

I returned to my library table and, sweeping the physiology notes aside, drew two swift spirals on a sheet of paper. I thought best in pictures. My illumination had come as a visual image. I had to catch it while it was fresh in my mind. As I stared at the spirals on paper I realised if one vortex of energy was accelerating relative to the other, one could be acting as a bubble of space in which the other was moving. In that moment of inspiration I also saw the vortex of energy as the origin of both space and matter. It was simple; the tight vortex energy at the centre was the massive particle and space was the sparse spread of vortex energy into infinity. As I pored over my picture it dawned on me that each vortex presents a three-dimensional extension of space through which other vortices can move. That was relativity! I saw vortex energy extending from a body, setting up shells of space around it. I sketched a picture of a man surrounded by an aura. This was his bubble of space. From this picture it dawned on me that we are not confined by our bodies but extend way beyond. We are in touch with everyone else through our bubbles of space; and subtly they touch us. I realised why no one is an island. We may appear to be separated but in reality we are all connected.

One moment of illumination led to another on that awesome afternoon in the library of Queen Elisabeth College. Major realisations raced into my mind. Obviously, as a form of energy, space would be divided into particles. The bubbles I had imagined were particles of space; I had a quantum theory for space. I got up and walked back to the library window buzzing with excitement. Looking out at the glistening street I was looking at a new world. Had I found a way to integrate quantum theory and relativity?

I knew there was a chasm between those two major pillars of modern science. What excited me was the possibility of a new approach to quantum theory could emerge from the principle Einstein used to develop his general theory of relativity; the very theory which was at odds with quantum theory.

I am still in awe of those magnetic moments of discovery. My recall of the library shelves, the windows even the smell of the book is vivid. The memory of looking over the brick wall surrounding the college into the streets of Kensington fills me with nostalgia even to this day.

On that day I walked back to my table considering one vortex relative to another. If every vortex swirled in the space provided by every other vortex, for atoms the rule would be: *Love thy neighbour for thy very existence!*

I couldn't wait to tell Father Ronan at the Carmelite Church on Kensington Church Street. He was attempting to recruit me for the Carmelites and would be excited to hear that the primary commandment of Christ, that we *love one another*, was the relativity law, the primary law in physics upon which all other laws have their foundation.

In the action of the *universal law of love*, I visualised the energies of the Universe, streaming in and out of each other in a mutual giving and receiving. In those sublime moments I was appreciating the principle place of love in physics.

I concluded, "We set up vibrations in our extensions of space by our thoughts and these frequencies extend into infinity, they touch everyone and have a subtle influence on everything. This is how the collective thoughts of humanity affect the entire Universe."

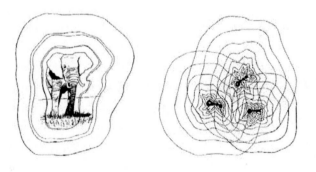

Bubbles of Space drawn by Anna

Chapter 11
Streams of Time

People who ignore things are ignorant

Michael Ash

My new theory for space had to include time. I paced the streets of Kensington pondering on time. Walking in Holland Park inspired me. The woodland setting helped me to simplify my thoughts and touch my centre. I would often go there to think.

I considered the events in our world that we experience as the passage of time. We take our measure of time from the regular movements of Earth and Moon; the spin of the Earth on its axis providing twenty-four hour days its orbit round the sun counting the years and the movement of the Moon lunar months.

I thought a lot about Einstein. If he was right and time was in continuum with space then time would have something to do with vortices of energy. But I couldn't perceive of another dimension in the spherical vortex apart from the three dimensions of space. Where was the fourth dimension of time? I thought very deeply but made no progress. Then one day it came to me during an unrelated conversation over tea.

Mrs. Weir enjoyed a tease over the evening meal. On one occasion she asked me to guess what the meat on my plate was. I said rissoles. She said it definitely wasn't rissoles and waited until I was eating heartily before telling me, with impish delight, that it was brains. I put down my knife and fork in disgust. I couldn't finish my plate. She then challenged me as a nutritionist saying a plate of brains was a good, inexpensive source of protein!

One day the twinkle in her eye wasn't over a disgusting dish of brains, it was about the Pope.

"David, as a nutritionist and a Catholic how do you reconcile the Pope's ban on contraceptives with over-population and malnutrition?"

"Mrs. Weir, when I was a boy in Harley Street. Bertrand Russell challenged my mother with the same question and he even reprimanded her for having so many children and not using contraceptives. My mother's immediate reply was, 'It was a pity your mother didn't use a contraceptive!'

When Mrs. Weir finished laughing I continued, "In response to his comment my mother did try the cap but I found it and pranced into the crowded waiting room with it on my head. Ma was so embarrassed she never used it again so I suppose I have to take some responsibility for the size of our family."

Mrs. Weir asked the age differences between my brothers and sisters

"Well," I said, doing some rough calculations in my head, "There was a year and five months between Jenny and Tim, then I followed Tim by a year and a week. Simon followed me by a year and about six months then Stephen arrived a year and five months after that..."

"You poor mother," Mrs. Weir interrupted, "She had no break, there was hardly more than a year between any of you! Mind the one thing in favour of large Catholic families like yours is that as fast as one of you grew out of your clothes there was always another behind to grow into them..."

I put down my knife and fork again, not in revulsion but exhilaration. I was so excited I could hardly finish my meal. "You're a genius, and absolute genius. You are brilliant!" I exclaimed.

"What have I done?" she asked with genuine interest.

"You have just explained time."

"How have I done that?"

"It's what you said about the children growing through their clothes. Why did I never see it before? It is so simple, so obvious!"

It wasn't simple and obvious to my surrogate mum.

"David I haven't got a clue what you are talking about. Go and clarify your thoughts then come back to me with the answer," she said abruptly, clearing away my plate.

It was a clear evening in early May. I headed for Holland Park to sort my thoughts.

What I had seen over supper was the vortex as a family. The clothes for each year that Mrs. Weir spoke of were the levels of intensity of energy at set distances from the centre of the vortex. The children growing through each set of clothes were the spheres of vortex energy growing through the levels of intensity.

The clothes for each year were continually in use because there was always a child wearing them; but from one year to the next it was never the same child. Likewise at each distance from the centre of the vortex there was always the same intensity of energy. These immutable levels of intensity were the immortal shells of space.

As fast as one child put down a set of clothes the next one would pick them up. As fast as a sphere of energy grew through a level of intensity another sphere was behind it

127

growing or shrinking – depending on the sign of charge – to take its place.

The scent of bluebells filled the air of Holland Park. As I walked by the statue of Lord Holland I spoke to the imagined gaggle of spectacled students running after me, eager for eternal knowledge. "You must realise," I explained enthusiastically, "Space is not the vortex of energy. Space is a level of intensity of energy at a distance from the centre of the vortex. These levels are shells. They are stable and give space the same stasis as matter. The flow of dynamic energy through static shells of space is time."

A courting couple hurried past, throwing me an apprehensive glance as the long light of evening lingered to light fresh leaves in shades of pink and gold. Another thought sprang into mind: If time is the flow of real energy through the illusionary shells space, then time is the relationship between the real and the unreal!

I also thought, because light flows in a single direction from source to destination, the propagation of light through space sets up the flow of time from the past through the present and into the future.

The call of a peacock broke the silence of twilight. I headed for home.

As I walked back I pondered on the 'illusion of forms' created by the vortex. I thought about the ripples and whirlpools in the stream in Cornwall. They only existed when the water flowed through them. If ever the stream ran dry, these transitory forms of water would vanish. The forms of matter and space were also an illusion; only the energy flowing through them was real.

Understanding time, I realised the illusion of maya spoken of in Yogic philosophy. I saw the Universe as a vast unfolding dream of transient forms that were ultimately dissolved in time.

A week or so later I wandered in on a group of students watching a television programme in the student union. It was a nature program on big cats. I had walked in at the point where they were showing a film of the movements of a black cat slowed down and then a real time film of a panther. It was virtually impossible to distinguish between the cat and the panther.

That sort of thing kept happening to me. It was uncanny. I never had time to watch television. I was far too busy. Then by pure chance I caught just the programme I needed to see. Those few moments of television led me to my next insight. I realised that size had an influence on time.

As always I walked into Holland Park to consider the revelation. It was a lovely summer evening again in late May, warm after a day of brilliant sunshine. In the slanting rays of the setting sun the atmosphere was full of insects dancing the still air with the celebration of life. I looked at the insects in a new light. I realised their activity only appeared jerky because they were smaller than me. A new term came to me as I watched them; *zones of time*.

Once again I was speaking in the illusionary lecture theatre: "The zone of time is influenced by the size of space."

I picked up a mayfly and held it up to my imagined audience. "This insect lives for only a day to man but in its own time zone it is a lifetime. An hour to man would be an aeon to the atom."

As I wandered through the park, past the rose garden and down the meadow toward the Commonwealth Institute I noticed Jupiter had appeared in the twilight sky. Strolling down Kensington High Street I imagined I was a giant and the planets were my stepping-stones through space. I pictured myself leaping from Saturn to Jupiter and then onto Mars. I visualised the Earth spinning like a blue and white football. I imagined what fun it would be to kick it out of its orbit and send it flying off into outer space. Then I thought better of that. Aha, it could be a useful timepiece where it was; a perfect little clock. The terrestrial spin that microscopic man used to count his days I could use to count my minutes. The orbit of the moon, man's month would be my gigantic hour. Each circumnavigation around the sun would count for me as a day.

I realised then that if God were big enough to look down on the universe, days to God would count as billions of years to man. In a stroke I had resolved a fundamental disagreement between religion and science. According to the Bible, God created the world in seven days but science has proved the evolution of the Universe and life forms occurred over billions of years. As with Newton and Einstein, the conflict between religion and science was caused by nothing more than a different point of view.

Newton with his Bible believed in a God looking down on heavenly bodies in space attracted to each other by gravity. Agnostic Einstein took the position of man looking into the heavens. He considered the motion of one body relative to another.

It is all a matter of relativity, I surmised, everyone sees the world from his or her own standpoint and judges others from that limited perspective. That is the primary source of conflict on the little blue and white football that floats silently in space. So much conflict in history has been over different points of view. The only lasting resolution to conflict was the universal law of love embodied in Einstein's understanding of space and time; that everything exists and moves relative to everything else in the Cosmos. I concluded the law of time is also the law of love: Everything is interdependent. Sadly, back at home in Cornwall, time was running out on Tim.

One Saturday in July 1970, an open top Morris pulled into our drive. At the wheel was a girl I vaguely knew from college and beside her was another who I didn't know. As I leant over the passenger door offering them both a very warm welcome there was a mad scramble on the gravel behind me. Two brothers were racing to the car and Tim made it by a head. Blocking the way for Simon, his beaten sibling, he staked his claim.

The two drop dead gorgeous girls were staying in a caravan down at Rock and invited us to join them. We needed no persuasion. Tim was finger swinging the keys to our Moggy as they spoke. Grabbing a few essentials and dashing to our car we followed in hot pursuit.

We were greeted at Rock by a watery sun and a freshening breeze. Tim wasted no time in hiring a sailing dingy for the four of us and within our allocated hour the girls were soaked by flying spray as Tim steered a course to maximize their screams. I could see a master was at work. As he was my older brother I let him steer the day.

A ferry trip to Padstow for cream teas followed and then back across the Camel estuary to the cinema at Polzeath for a showing of *The Graduate*. Because of his infirmity Tim hadn't had a girl friend for years. He was squeezing every succulent moment out of the God sent opportunity.

Sunday morning was wet and wild but in the cosy caravan no care was given to the weather as cooked breakfast was served. Somehow or other the conversation strayed onto the subject of death. One of the girls spoke of her fear of dying. Tim replied he had no fear of death as he had to live with it constantly. He even declared he was prepared to die tomorrow!

The party broke soon after breakfast as the girls had to pack and get back to London. Two happy brothers drove home in satisfied silence.

Monday woke grey and murky. The wind had subsided and the promise of good surf was greeted in the early morning by Tim, Simon and Peter. The lot had fallen on me to stay behind to meet Mike Preller and discuss the next stage of the building, which we boys had taken over due to the lack of funds. I was in the caravan working on my physics when a car roared into the drive and braked hard on the gravel. It was the desperation in Mike Preller's voice as he shouted, "David, David", that told me. I don't know how I knew but immediately I knew my brother Tim was dead.

Mike was in tears when I ran down to him. From my premonition I was able to offer consolation as we raced down to the Haven. Tim had already been taken away in an ambulance when I arrived. Simon and Peter were inconsolable.

Through their tears they told me Tim had caught a wave and was pushing his board back out for another when he collapsed in the shallows. By the time they reached him he was floating headfirst on the water. They had pulled him onto the beach and attempted resuscitation (we were all trained in surf life saving) but to no avail. Tim was pronounced dead by the paramedics when the ambulance arrived.

Ma and Pa were away at the time. I managed to reach them by phone to call them home. Word spread quickly and as distressed friends and family members either phoned or came round, I was able to reassure them everything was all right. With that premonition had come a deep sense of peace and strength to handle the situation. When parents arrived they said the doctors had warned them Tim would not last. His death occurred within six months of the prognosis so they had been prepared. He was given the dignity of 'death by drowning' on his death certificate; an appropriate epitaph for a surfer who was living his life to the full right up until his very last moment.

We dug Tim's grave in the rocky churchyard of St Genny's on the cliffs. The serene view out to sea was spectacular. It was a fitting place to lay our brother to rest and I wrote a song to commemorate his passing:

Have you ever let real stillness for a moment be your all,
Have you ever stopped a moment and lived at all,
Have you ever stopped to ponder but never thought at all,
Have you ever stopped to wonder why ever you were born.

In the bustle of living we never live at all,
Our lives may come together but on life we never call,
And in every single moment of our lives flying by,
There's a wonder all the words ever spoken can't describe.

So busy talking, so busy thinking, so busy toiling for a dime,
So busy doing, so busy dying but when we die we leave behind, all
the people, all the money, all the houses, all behind, and as the mists
of time go swirling, of our lives we've spent our time.

To late to wonder on the meaning and the purpose of life,
To late to see a single dewdrop in the morning sun alight
To late to feel in every moment such a joy unending bliss
To late to find the door to heaven in the breath we left behind

So don't squander life's precious moments,
Keep searching till you find,
The way that leads to heaven,
Through the heart, deep inside

Chapter 12
Explaining Angels

"Stars are angels disguised in light."

Michael Ash

When I moved to London my parents sent Mary to a convent school to get her away from boys. But undaunted by the nun with a baseball bat snoozing outside the dorm, Roger the Dodger nipped up the fire escape, through the window of Mary's cubicle and fathered Claire. Despite the fact that Claire was an angel - only angels are conceived in convents - Mary was expelled as soon as her school uniform began to bulge.

I supported Mary in her teenage pregnancy but foresaw days of difficulty for her if she married Roger so young. She was only fifteen for heaven's sake. I expressed my feelings for her in a song:

Mary, Mary listen to the wind a blowing,
A wind from the arid plain of life,
That wind can strip you naked,
Taking all, leaving only strife,
Your love to be forsaken,
Your home and treasures taken,
Mary, Mary only then will you seek the light.

Mary, Mary rivers flow from mountains a crumbling,
Crimson waters stained with the blood of all,

Lovers and brothers Mary,
Gone, taken by the sword.
Your love to be forsaken,
Your home and treasures taken,
Mary, Mary only then is your choice outright.

Mary, Mary the spring of love has come to you at last,
Lush green bursting out of dust,
Life is rich and much is given,
But all things go if in them you trust.
Your love to be forsaken,
Your home and treasures taken,
Mary, Mary only then are you free for flight.

Mary, Mary listen to the wind a blowing,
A wind from the arid plain of life,
That wind can strip you naked,
Taking all, leaving only strife,
Your love to be forsaken,
Your home and treasures taken,
Mary, Mary only then will you see the light.

I was about to encounter my maiden sister's namesake, the maiden – mistranslated from Hebrew as virgin - who fell pregnant at the same age two thousand years ago. It began when I met Nimal Mendis, a recording artist from Sri Lanka who had recently appeared on the BBC *Top of the Pops*. He introduced Stephen, Simon and I to his music publisher, Joe Roncoroni who signed us up. We started recordings at the Lansdowne Studio in Holland Park Avenue, a two-minute walk from my lodgings. It was the fast winding spools on the studio tape decks that helped me link electric charge and gravity to the vortex but my interest in physics didn't impress Joe Roncoroni. When it became clear to him we had no intention of dropping out of college for a music career he decided to drop us.

Nimal had returned to Colombo but before departing he lent me a book on the Marian apparitions at Garabandal in Spain. The book recorded that on June 18 1961; in the foothills of the Cantabrain of Northern Spain, four girls were playing in the outskirts the mountain village *San Sebastian de Garabandal,* when the air was rent with a clap of thunder. Thinking a storm was approaching the girls finished their game and started to head for home. All four girls froze in their tracks when, at the top a rocky track called the Cuadro, they saw a boy standing in a brilliant orb of light. Dressed in a blue robe, he appeared to be about ten. He smiled at the girls and then vanished.

Conchita, Loli and Jacinta were twelve and Maria Cruz eleven so when they attempted to tell their parents what they had seen they were packed off to bed for fabricating a fanciful story.

However, over the next few days the boy in blue appeared again to the girls in the Cuadro. Their experience on these occasions was that they were completely surrounded in light and were aware of nothing but him. He said nothing but merely smiled before disappearing.

Curious villagers began to follow the girls and witnessed them fall suddenly on their knees with their heads thrown back, their faces joyful and radiant. The four girls were in a state of ecstasy and the village was abuzz with excitement.

On July 1st the boy appeared again and spoke. He said he was the Archangel Michael and would return the following day with Mary and that they would appear to the girls in a grove of pines up in the hills above the Cuadro.

The girls were perplexed. The boy bore no resemblance to the statue of Michael in the village church. Despite their doubts word went out of Garabandal like wildfire. From early morning a steady stream of people made their way from the surrounding district up the rocky mountain track to the village. By the time the girls headed for the grove of pines for their 6:00 p.m. rendezvous with the celestial visitors the village was thronging and hundreds followed them up the Cuadro.

The girls fell into rapture for a few minutes. When they returned to normal they said a girl around the age of sixteen in a white dress and blue mantle had appeared. She was carrying a baby. The boy was there with another just like him and they stood either side of the young mother. Nothing was said. They just smiled at the girls and then vanished.

That was the beginning of thousands of apparitions at Garabandal between 1961 and 1965. The young mother with her baby appeared to the four Spanish children almost every day and often at night. The girls were very relaxed with her and came to regard her as a friend. She addressed herself as Our Lady of Mount Carmel. This again surprised them because dressed in white and blue she didn't resemble the statue of Our Lady of Mount Carmel in their church portrayed with a brown robe.

Apart from the strange apparitions the girls grew up as normal teenagers, interested in clothes, boys and music on the radio. During the four years doctors and scientists from many countries witnessed the apparitions and documented their reactions. They were impressed by their normality. There was no sign of hysteria, neurosis, psychosis or piety. Whilst in rapture the girls were impervious to pain inflicted by pins and cigarette lighters. Their bodies were in a state of rigour and were unusually heavy. The strongest men in the village had difficulty lifting them. Yet they would frequently levitate and move backwards over rough ground faster than people following could run forwards. They would also float rapidly on their knees or traverse the rocky Cuadro at night in winter, when it was covered in ice or fast flowing water at running speed when followers could barely stumble along behind. Also, while in ecstasy the girls, who could normally only speak Spanish, would sometimes recite prayers in Latin or Greek. This occurred when priests were in the crowd.

Impressed by the reports, Stephen, Simon Peter and I decided to visit Garabandal. We were struck by the simplicity of the sleepy village. Of the four girls only Loli was still living in the village, tending her father's shop. Two of the others were married and living in other villages. Conchita, married to an American doctor, had moved to the U.S.A.

Loli was very pleasant and answered our questions with patience. She chewed gum and laughed a lot and there was no sign of pretension or piety. She said the apparitions were a fading memory but she missed the intimacy with the beautiful Lady and she was comforted by her return once a year on her birthday.

I was interested in the apparitions both as a Catholic and because of my mystic approach to physics. The appearance of the angel as a boy without wings impressed me. He was obviously more concerned to put the girls at their ease than appear like an angel with wings and the fact he looked so different to the statue in the church confirmed they weren't imagining things.

The apparitions of Garabandal supported my predictions of the existence of realms of energy beyond the speed of light in which intelligent beings could see us even if we couldn't see them. This was clear from the conversations the girls had with the Blessed Maiden Mary. She was very aware of everything going on in their lives, the village and the world beyond.

I reasoned that if our world is formed out of particles of energy existing at the speed of light, other worlds could be formed out of speeds faster than light. If that were so then our world would be a part of these worlds because slow speeds are part of faster speeds.

As a boy I had been told that angels are all around us but we are not aware of them because they are moving too fast. I reasoned it wasn't that the angel was moving faster than light, rather the intrinsic speed of energy forming the angel was moving too fast to be visible and tangible in our world. Physical light would not reflect off the angel's body neither would it interact with matter because he would not be in our space-time.

I deduced that from the Mincowski Diagram. Mincowski worked with on Einstein the mathematics of relativity and formulated a diagram illustrating conclusions of Einstein's amazing theory. One principle was that movement faster than light could not be contained in physical space and time.

I argued that vortices and waves could set up space and time in other dimensions and form other worlds that would be just like our own. The laws of physics would be the same; only the speed of the energy would differ. If Michael and Mary appeared with bodies dressed in robes, then obviously they were formed of atomic matter like our own.

When the girls encountered Mary they could only see her in light and no one else saw the apparition. This suggested to me their consciousness was drawn into another dimension. Only when the angel first appeared did the celestial beings enter our world. That was when the girls saw him at the head of the Cuadro in an orb of light within the landscape.

I read the report of a farmer who was working in the fields on the afternoon Michael first appeared. He said he saw a flash of light strike the head of the Cuadro and heard the roll of thunder. He reported it as unusual because the lightning came out of a cloudless sky. I concluded that when the angel first arrived he could have decelerated the speed of energy in every subatomic vortex of his body to appear in our world. His sudden disappearance would have been a reversal of this process. Accelerating the speed of energy in every vortex in the atoms of his boyish body it would have vanished out of physical space and time.

The idea of moving matter in and out of space-time by changing the intrinsic speed of energy in the atom was useful to me. I used it subsequently to explain a whole host of paranormal phenomena including, many years later, the materializations of the Indian mystic, Sathya Sai Baba.

Back in London after the sublime summer, I proved by experiment I wasn't an angel! I had a project to complete for my nutrition course and my tutor emphasised it would play a vital part in my final marks. Each student was given a special diet, chosen at random. My lot fell on a high fat, low protein diet. I was issued with a set of weighing scales and a ten-gallon, plastic can and told to work out what I was going to eat for two or three days according to the diet. During that period every bit of food and drink had to be weighed and measured and all urine had to be collected in the plastic container for analysis in the lab.

At the end of the period we had to calculate the nitrogen content of the food we had eaten and assay the urine in the lab to ascertain our nitrogen output. We then had to write a report on our nitrogen balance and submit it, typed like a thesis.

Our tutors stressed the importance of not going out or away during the period of the trial as we were embarking on a scientific study to be taken seriously and not be compromised by usual student activities that might impair the results. That was not a problem for me. With my work on the vortex physics I had become a virtual hermit. I had no girlfriend in London at the time and had no money for pubs or eating out so there was little chance of my being tempted off my diet. The only danger lay in Mrs. Weir's meals so I announced that I would feed myself for the next few days.

I went up to Notting Hill Gate and purchased provisions. For my first lunch on the diet I had rye crisp breads spread thick with butter, plastered with strawberry jam and covered in double dairy cream. Delicious! For supper I had two slices of granary bread spread thick with butter, plastered with strawberry jam, covered in cream followed by some grapes and an apple. The sight, next morning, of bread and butter, jam and cream on my bedside table made me feel queasy so I decided to skip breakfast. Armed with my jerry can and scales, feeling hungry and a bit demoralised, I set out for college.

As I pushed open the gate a parp-parp sounded, behind me. I turned to see an open sports car coming down the Square. A couple of blokes in woolly hats were grinning at me through the windscreen. I couldn't make out who they were.

"Hello David," the driver called out, "It's me, your cousin Andrew. This is my business partner Bill."

"Hello David," echoed Bill in a loud, bass voice.

"Andrew, what on Earth are you doing here?" I exclaimed. This was a totally unexpected surprise. I hadn't seen Andrew for years.

"We're off to Hastings," he replied, "Do you want come?"

The sun was rising high over the rooftops in a clear blue sky. I could almost smell the salt on the wind and hear the haunting call of the gulls. There was nothing I wanted to do more at that moment than buzz off to Hastings but I couldn't possibly go. I had been warned not to go anywhere for the duration of the project. I had to be firm and sensible for once in my life. I had to say no.

"I would love to come but I am in the middle of an important project so I will have to say no. Thanks anyway for inviting me."

"Come on David." The wicked cat like gin on Andrew's face was stretched from ear to ear.

"Yes, come on," added Bill with a foxy smile half hidden behind a hooked pipe.

Pinocchio knew he had to go to school and would get into trouble if he went off with the fox and cat but the promise of fun and adventure, freedom and the open road, spinning along in that sports car to Hastings was all too much for him.

"What about these?" Pinocchio held up the scales and cumbersome plastic can.

"Bring them along," shouted the fox and cat in unison. Andrew was already out of the car stuffing a cushion behind the gear stick and Bill had the boot open ready to stow the paraphernalia.

Planted firmly on the cushion, between two rascals, a woolly hat jammed on his woodenhead, Pinocchio absconded.

On the way to Hastings we dropped in on Bill's sister.

"Time for breakfast," said Andrew.

"I could eat a horse," sounded Bill.

Bill's sister was that sort of warm woman who always had a larder full to bursting coupled with a vocation to satisfy the appetites of men. Her kitchen was soon full of laughter, chatter and the delicious smell of sizzling bacon.

"Are you sure you won't have a cooked breakfast?"

"No thank you very much," I groaned, "two rounds of toast with butter and jam, cereal and a dob of cream will suffice."

Two slices of bread or toast contained all the protein I was allowed in a meal. Eating them did nothing to appease my hunger and the bowl of cornflakes and cream left me totally dissatisfied.

"You've got to have a proper breakfast," declared Andrew, tucking into his fried eggs, bacon, sausages, tomatoes, fried bread and mushrooms.

"You'll fade away," intoned Bill, over his plate full of traditional English breakfast.

I was desperate. Then I had a brain wave. If I weighed the forbidden food, I could work out its nitrogen content later and subtract it from my end results. Nobody would know the difference.

Andrew and Bill agreed that was a splendid idea.

"A real brain-box, just like your Pa," said Andrew

"A budding Einstein," agreed Bill.

Two eggs, four rashers of bacon, a sausage, two tomatoes, six mushrooms and a slice of bread were soon weighed, fried and eaten.

We arrived in Hastings Old Town just before lunch and began to hunt in the junk shops for chests of drawers and tables. Andrew and Bill were in the pine stripping business and traveled the country searching for furniture. After rummaging around for a while we began to feel peckish.

"Let's have fish and chips," suggested Bill.

"Yes, it would be a crime to visit Hastings and not have fish and chips," Andrew affirmed.

I soon had my scales out on the fish and chip counter to weigh a large slab of cod. "This will be easy enough to calculate," I thought, "Cod is almost pure protein!"

For the rest of the afternoon I trailed along after Andrew and Bill, my scales in one hand and my ten-gallon jerry can in the other, as they plunged in and out of the second-hand shops in the old town. Eventually we ended up on the beach waiting for the pubs to open. Hunting for junk furniture was thirsty work and there was no way Andrew and Bill were going to leave without a little tipple to drink.

We had just settled into a pub and were downing a pint of beer when Andrew and Bill spotted a blackboard advertising a most economic plate of steak and chips. "Well," I thought, "I may as well hang for a steer as a calf," so out came the scales and in went the steak and chips, washed down with another pint of beer.

Two pints of beer were about my limit. For Andrew and Bill, two pints were starters.

"Come on David, have another one," said Andrew placing a third pint in front of me.

"My turn," said Bill, who didn't seem to hear my flat refusal to drink anymore as he went off to fetch the fourth round of beers.

The room began to spin and I was bursting. Picking up my can I tottered off to the gents. Andrew and Bill thought that was a good idea and ambled along after me. I did my best to pee into the can but lost my aim. Andrew and

Bill stood there watching as I spilt more urine than I collected.

"Here, let me have a go," said Andrew grabbing the can from me. Being more used to drink than me his aim was straight and true, he didn't spill a drop. I did try to get the can back from him but at that point I was overwhelmed with uncontrollable laughter and by the time I recovered Andrew had passed the receptacle onto Bill to add his contribution.

Chapter 13
The Dog in Space

Even if the whole world is against you it doesn't mean you are wrong."

Michael Ash

If you happened by Campden Hill Square, in the early 1970s and saw a lanky lad dragged for his morning walk at the end of a lead by a small brown sausage-dog it was me. The dog was the Weir's dachshund Johannes. He took me out for regular walks to keep me fit and led me, not only to practically every lamp-post in Campden Hill square, but to a revolutionary understanding of Einstein's special theory of relativity.

One lunch break in early summer I returned to my room to collect some books on nutrition. I bounded up the front steps munching on an apple, unlocked the front door, threw it open and burst in. To this day I will never forget the extraordinary spectacle I beheld in the Weir's hall and the impact that it had on me.

Johannes had piles. In order to keep him on his bed in the hall, Mrs Weir had rolled him up tightly in a red blanket so he looked more like a sausage roll than a sausage dog.

Hearing me come to the door he assumed he was going for a walk. Somehow he managed to wriggle free his front paws and launch himself onto the floor. I was confronted with the sight of Johannes pulling himself across to me by his front paws. The blanket was still wrapped round his tummy and he was dragging it along behind him. It was obvious he wanted to get out of the blanket but he couldn't extract himself from the roll because it moved with him wherever he went.

As I watched the antics of the dog in its blanket I had an illumination. I pictured Johannes as the body of matter and the wrap as his bubble of space. I realised that the matter couldn't move relative to its own space because this moved with it wherever it went. In that apple munching moment of enlightenment I reinterpreted the principle idea in Einstein's special theory of relativity - why the velocity of light always appears to be the same regardless of the movement of the observer.

A scientist measuring the velocity of light can only measure the velocity of those photons of light, which come to him. As they do so they would be traveling in his bubble of space, which, like the dog's blanket wrap, would be moving with him wherever he went. The measured velocity of light in his own space would be unaffected by his own movement.

I had a first hand encounter with relativity from a painful experience attending my beehives in Cornwall. I never bothered with full protective gear. I just stuffed a bee veil in the neck of my shirt. It was usually sufficient but one thundery day the bees were in a particularly feisty mood and began a ferocious attack. I ran but a couple of determined workers got in under my veil and no matter how fast I moved they stung me on my face!

The bees represented photons of light and the bee veil my bubble of space. If I ran fast enough I could get away from the bees outside my veil. However, I couldn't escape the angry bees inside my veil zooming in on my ears and nose because I carried them along with me as I ran.

I found my bubble theory for space also explained Einstein's general theory of relativity, published in 1915.

Einstein predicted that space-time was distorted by the mass of the sun. He used the analogy of a heavy ball indenting a sheet of rubber. He suggested that light from distant stars passing close to the sun would appear to be deflected as it moved through the curved space.

A solar eclipse of the sun in 1919 provided an opportunity to test Einstein's prediction. Professor Arthur Eddington of the Royal Society organised two expeditions to test the theory. His plan was to photograph the sky during the eclipse and compare these with photographs of the same sky at night. The plates from the Africa expedition were spoilt but those from the back-up expedition on the other side of the Atlantic were perfect and showed an apparent displacement of the stars around the sun precisely as predicted.

The Royal Society published their findings and overnight Einstein became the most celebrated scientist in the world. Coming just after the end of World War I, the vindication of a German scientist's prediction by an English scientific expedition was timely and well received worldwide.

However, my father warned me about Einstein's general theory of relativity. He said while it was brilliant it could not be true because of its great complexity. He referred to the groundbreaking work of Rutherford and drummed into my head Lord Rutherford's axiom: *These fundamental things have got to be simple.*

One day my father directed an alternative expedition to the one that landed the general theory. His expedition led me to an alternative to Einstein's theory; though not to the celebrity status. But then his expedition was slightly less prestigious than the one launched by the Royal Society.

Roundabouts were proliferating in England and Pa didn't like them as they impeded his 'Toad-like' progress on the open road. So one day, with me and my brother Tim on board, he attempted to drive our little Austin Seven right over one – he would never have done that with his Bentley! The back axle broke and we pushed the unfortunate vehicle, with its bicycle-spoke wheels, into a ditch and hitched home. The lesson for me that day was that cars are supposed follow roads. If the road happens to go round a roundabout the car has to go round too.

From my 'Bubble space' theory it was obvious that the space extending from the sun would be an extension of the shape of the sun. The shape of space extending from the sun had to be concentric spheres. When I was thinking about Einstein's general theory, I recalled our escapade in the Austin Seven. I reasoned that just as motor cars usually follow the curvature of the road round a roundabout so the light from stars, passing close to the sun, would follow the curvature of space round the sun. Einstein proposed that space round the sun is curved because space-time is distorted by the mass of the sun. I contended that the space round the sun is curved because it is an extension of the sun. The effect is the same; only the account is different.

Einstein used his idea about space-time distortion to account for gravity. I had a completely different account for the way space caused gravity. Mine came through re-reading the fairy tales from my childhood. And in the end, like Einstein, I proved my vortex account for gravity as a valid scientific theory by successfully predicting the outcome of a future astronomical observation.

Chapter 14
The Gravity of the Matter

"People are blind who deny the existence of things they cannot see."

Michael Ash

Pa read us Hans Christian Anderson when we were children but I preferred Alice and the White Rabbit. My preference was to pay dividends. When I was at college there was a lot of excitement about the physics of 'Alice in Wonderland' so I re-read the story searching for parallels with my own interpretation of physics. I was not disappointed.

Alice chasing a white rabbit that kept looking at his clock was a clue for time. The rabbit was in a tearing hurry as though things were speeding up. That fitted with the acceleration toward the centre of the vortex. Then Alice drank a potion that caused her to shrink. I knew immediately that was suggestive of the contraction of space toward the centre of the vortex particle. Her journey down the tunnel took her into a looking glass world and that was the most significant clue of all because it shouted at me 'the mirror symmetry of matter and antimatter is down a tunnel and into the small.' This was confirmed by Alice meeting the identical twins Tweedledum and Tweedledee in the looking glass world who 'agreed to have a battle.' That to my mind was obviously the 'pair-particle' annihilation of matter and antimatter. The clues were all in. All I had to do was figure them out.

Mrs. Weir had cut an article out of the *Daily Telegraph* for me. It featured a theory from Tel Aviv University, which pictured the Universe as a pair of trousers. One trouser leg was equivalent to the Universe of matter. The other leg represented a Universe of antimatter. Just as one leg in a pair of trousers is a mirror image of the other, so each half of the universe would be a precise duplicate of the other.

From Alice in Wonderland I found the clue to where the antimatter half of the Universe was; *down a tunnel and shrinking through the smallest door leads to a looking glass world.*

I realised the Universe of antimatter had to exist down the tunnel of the vortex through the smallest realms of space. It had to be beyond the centre of the vortex!

Next came Pa, the March Hare! His reverence for Rutherford had inculcated in me since childhood that his laws and discoveries were sacrosanct. Rutherford had proposed a conservation law for charge that whenever a particle with a positive charge was created, an equal but negative charge also came into being and whenever a positive charge was annihilated a negative charge was destroyed. Pa's influence over me was crucial at this point.

I was appalled at the popular idea in mainstream cosmology that in the beginning the Universe came into being with slightly more matter than antimatter and all the anti-matter annihilated with most of the matter and the remnant is the Universe we witness today.

Pa had taught me not to heed that sort of silly nonsense. He said, "David, people are blind who deny the existence of things they cannot see." Pa taught me to trust Rutherford. If Rutherford said for every particle of matter in existence there had to be an equal but opposite particle of antimatter then that was law!

I told Pa I knew where the antimatter was! I said that if he could drink the 'drink-me drink' and shrink into the smallest space inside the vortex, eventually, like Alice chasing the white rabbit he would pop through the tiny door, the zero space point at its centre. Then like Alice he would step into the looking glass world; the world of antimatter.

I was standing with him on Congdons Bridge adjacent to our land in Cornwall. I was on vacation and we were on our way up the valley to visit a neighbour, Liz Cummins. Looking down at the busy stream I began to relay to my father the model I was developing for the universe.

"Look Pa," I said, "Water from under the bridge appears to come out of nowhere, and then in the distance as the stream takes a bend it vanishes again. However, if we follow the stream down to the Haven we will see the water flow into the ocean. Then as clouds sweep in up the valley from the sea and rain from the clouds falls on the hills, the water returns through the springs back into the stream.

"In like manner," I explained as we ambled up the lane, "Energy would flow endlessly through the vortices of matter and antimatter, as part of a universal cycle of energy much like water in the water cycle. The infinity of space is the circle between matter and antimatter."

"I'm not following you," said Pa opening the gate to the footpath by the orchard meadow leading up the valley.

"In your mind's eye, Pa, visualise the centre of a proton in your head. See the vortex energy expanding out of it as a minute bubble.

"Now, leap with your imagination onto the bubble as it commences its journey through the Universe. First imagine you are the size of the proton and then swell to the size of the nucleus. The spheres of vortex energy expanding out of all the other protons and neutrons merge to form this sphere expanding out of the nucleus.

"Now Pa, imagine the sphere growing out from the nucleus just as your original sphere grew out of the proton. There are larger spheres ahead of you and smaller ones behind, all expanding on the same journey. As your bubble of energy grows out into the atom, you see concentric spheres of energy traveling in the opposite direction. They are shrinking into all the electrons in the atom.

"You are now surrounded by millions of atoms in a cell. Now visualise yourself outside a brain cell. Still growing, your sphere of vortex energy is first as big as your brain and then your body. It is now no longer a sphere but is an extension of the shape of your body."

"The aura?" Pa interjected.

"Absolutely Pa."

"Go on with your story"

"OK Pa, now there are other people milling about you. Your own aura of vortex energy merges with theirs as it continues to grow. First they shrink and vanish as your vast bubble of energy grows to the size of the Earth and then the solar system. Still growing your sphere of vortex energy would become a mighty spheroid surrounding our galaxy. The enormous bubble would contain vortex energy from all the matter of the galaxy. It would then swell to encompass groups of galaxies until eventually it would be the largest sphere of space; the outermost frontier of the Universe."

"How would I know I had reached the frontier of the Universe?"

"Your sphere of energy would have stopped expanding and would begin to shrink.

"You would be shrinking back the way you came as galaxies grow up toward you. Then spinning down toward billions of stars you would be enveloped once again by the Milky Way.

"A point of light would race toward you expanding into the Sun but you would fly by it, zooming down towards a beautiful white and blue globe swelling up to meet you. You would see Africa and America but it is toward England that you would be drawn.

"Cornwall would appear in the patchwork landscape of England as you streak toward a distant speck."

"Cornwall isn't part of England!"

I ignored Pa's remark and continued, "As your sphere shrinks you recognise your own body which grows rapidly then bigger than a giant. What little hair you have would stand like trees as you shoot into your head, your sphere of energy shrinking into a single brain cell.

"Still shrinking you would enter the nucleus then hurtling into a DNA strand, an atom would swallow you whole. Spheres of energy would be expanding out of its orbiting vortices but Pa, they wouldn't be electrons; they would be antimatter positrons!

"You see Pa you would have shrunk back not the way you came but through the looking glass world of antimatter. Before you have time to wonder if you will be annihilated, you would be sucked down into an anti-proton and compressed into the single point of its centre, you would then pass through the zero space centre of the vortex and begin to grow again. Your sphere of vortex energy would start expanding up and out, as a proton. You would be right back where you started."

"I think I can see it now," Pa pondered thoughtfully, "The single, largest sphere of space is like the ocean and the countless atoms are like drops of rain."

"You've got it Pa, and the vortex energy spins between the smallest and the largest regions of space through matter and antimatter.

"Because every bit of matter is connected to a bit of antimatter at its centre, like Siamese twins, every form and action in the world of matter would have to be perfectly duplicated in the world of antimatter.

"There is a mirror image version of me beyond the inside of me out on a walk with an antimatter version of you Pa. The question is which is the real you and which is a mere reflection because my double would be speculating to your mirror that you are antimatter."

Pa straightening himself up; "Where are you leading David?"

"To a new theory for gravity, Pa!"

My father was suddenly interested. "Go on."

"Between matter and antimatter there is a force of attraction. This would cause an electric pull between the matter in our world and the antimatter in the looking glass world. The pull wouldn't be between you Pa and your antimatter shadow as you are inseparable. It would be between you and all other antimatter in existence. You can test this for yourself, right now."

"How?"

"Jump up Pa!"

Pa made a pathetic excuse of a jump.

"Come on Pa, jump up in the air properly."

Pa threw down his stick and took a leap. He stumbled and landed with a thump on his rump. I couldn't help but burst into laughter.

"What was that all about?" he asked offering me his hand.

"Gravity, Pa, gravity. You certainly beat the apple for impact. There is a pull between you and the antimatter Earth through the centre of the Earth," I explained pulling him up onto to his feet.

"At the same time you were pulling the Earth toward your centre but because she is more massive, she got the better of the tug.

"Now Pa there has to be a polar opposite of gravity," I continued enthusiastically as we continued to the Cummins. "This is a pull between matter and antimatter over the largest sphere of space. It is a decentralising pull acting on the largest things causing galaxies to accelerate apart and shoot off toward the outermost frontiers of space. The further galaxies are from us the faster they will be accelerating away from us…"

It was 1970 when I had that conversation with my father and 1995 before I published my prediction of the accelerating expansion of the Universe. Three years later, in 1998, the results of observations of supernova explosions in distant galaxies were published. They revealed that contrary to the expectations of the big bang theory; *the further galaxies are from us the faster they are accelerating from us.*

The biggest question in astronomy today is the cause of the anti-gravity force causing the accelerating expansion of the Universe. I provided my dad with an answer to that thirty nine years ago.

I don't know how much of that conversation Pa retained because he had other things on his mind. He had borrowed money from the bank to complete the building but was having difficulty meeting the monthly repayments from his meager practice so Ma nagged him away from his typewriter and sent him off to find a job. Pa went to Plymouth and signed up in the Royal Fleet Auxiliary. When his uniform arrived it was without trousers so Ma bought a pair of dress trousers from the Red Cross shop in Bude. They were a bit short in the leg so Steven and Simon celebrated in song:

> *Pa's gone a fishing and I wonder why,*
> *He's gone to join the navy all the sailors will die,*
> *The rats have left already they've got more sense,*
> *Been climbing out the funnels,*
> *And squeezing through the vents,*
> *Down on the dockyard you will see,*
> *The doctor with the hot-pants below his knee.*

> *The Royal Fleet Auxiliary what a laugh,*
> *I've come to thinking they're all daft*
> *Fancy employing such a funny bloke,*
> *The whole of the North Sea's going up in smoke,*
> *Down on the dockyard you will see,*
> *The doctor with the hot-pants below his knee.*

Pa was at sea when the West Country ITV Company based in Plymouth, then called *Westward TV,* sent up a film crew to make a programme of us living on the land, surfing and singing. *'Summer of the Ash Family'* was broadcast in 1972 on ITV and in New Zealand.

But it was difficult to write and sing songs with my brothers and sisters when we were all going our separate ways. Mary and Jenny were married and had started their families, Simon had secured a place at the London Hospital in Whitechapel to study dentistry and Steven had enrolled at the College of St Mark and St John in Chelsea to become a biology teacher. To rectify the situation Steven, Simon and I moved into shared digs during my last year at university. After I graduated in 1972 I left them in London and returned to Cornwall for a gap year. To begin with I moved onto a dairy farm with my girlfriend to help her milk the herd while her dad was in hospital. I was planning to go on an overland trip through Afghanistan to India and Sri Lanka with Peter but Pa, who had recently been decommissioned for injuring his back while attempting to teach the crew yoga - he never practiced it in his life - blocked my way. He had received a letter from Dunlop expressing an interest in my US patent as it incorporated conductive silicone rubber in its design. Pa insisted that I let Peter go on alone and stay behind to follow up the opportunity to develop my patent. He said I had my future to consider and would live to regret it if I missed the boat because of a fools errand to India. Although I wanted to go on the adventure with Peter I wasn't looking forward to leaving my girlfriend. I wanted to marry her and thought that through a deal with Dunlop I could win her hand. So I invested my savings on a trip to the Midlands to set up trials on my patent and building Ma a stable on the land. As always, the endeavour with Pa came to nothing. The trials were inconclusive so Dunlop dropped my patent and my girl friend dropped me. God was I miserable. I vowed never to work any more with Pa on his inventions and turning my back on Cornwall I went off to join the Carmelites.

Father Ronan arranged for me to enter the Carmelite Monastery at Boars Hill in Oxford. It was an ideal place to mend a broken heart and sort out confusion but the Carmelites weren't up for rehab. I had three relatively happy weeks there, and established beer brewing in the monastery, before I got kicked out. Father Abbot explained to me and another unsuccessful Postulant why. Those who melted into the community were allowed to stay. Those who stood out or simply didn't fit in were asked to leave. I wrote a hymn while I was in the cloister which may offer you a clue as to why I didn't fit into the monastic life:

> *I'm a monk,*
> *And I eat brown bread,*
> *And I live like the good Lord says,*
> *I'm a monk,*
> *And I eat brown bread,*
> *And I live like the good Lord says,*
> *But one thing's a paining me,*
> *It sure is a shame,*
> *I ain't allowed a woman,*
> *And man that's a strain,*
> *I'm a monk,*
> *And I have my bread,*
> *But I wish I had a woman instead.*
>
> *I'm a monk,*
> *And I eat brown bread,*
> *And I live like the good Lord says,*
> *I'm a monk,*
> *And I eat brown bread,*
> *And I live like the good Lord says,*
> *We have beer on Sundays,*
> *And wine on a feast,*
> *So why can't we have,*
> *A woman once a week,*
> *I'm a monk,*
> *And I have my bread,*
> *But I wish I had a woman instead.*
> *Oh I wish I had a woman instead.*

Chapter 15
Wrecker's Rights

Stir the crocks with a wooden spoon and you won't be asked to do the dishes again

Michael Ash

As an amateur pioneering scientist I had to be resourceful when it came to funding my research so without university grants or government funding what choice had I but to resort to the traditional way the Cornish raised cash in hard times!

In the late summer of 1973, fresh out of the monastery I was strolling through Bude in Cornwall when I spotted an Olivetti portable electric typewriter in a shop window for £100. I needed that typewriter as my old machine had just broken down; worn beyond repair through overuse. I couldn't make headway to express my ideas on paper without a typewriter but I had no money for the Olivetti.

Stephen didn't trust banks. He had entrusted me with £100 to tend while he went with his girlfriend on a motorbike holiday in France but I couldn't buy the typewriter with his money because I had already spent it.

My brother in law, Roger, had built a custom car out of an old Triumph Herald. He'd discarded the body, boot and bonnet replacing them with sheet of tin, painted chrome yellow that encircled the two front seats. There was no roof and a piece of hardboard on elastics covered the engine. The front wheel arches were adorned with a glorious pair of shiny chrome headlamps.

I had put out for a Noddy car when I was seven and at long last my prayer was answered. I was certain Stephen would have approved the investment of his £100, were it not for the unfortunate collision with a dustcart that landed Pa in a blackberry bush and left the Noddy car with an ugly dent.

Now Noddy had double trouble. He had to find £100 to repay Big Ears before he returned from the holiday on his motorbike as well as the £100 for the new typewriter. Munching blackberries in the bush, Pa suggested we pray the traditional Cornish prayer: *Lord I pray there won't be a wreck but if there is please let it be on my shore*

It wasn't long before our prayer was answered!

In was a late September night and a terrible storm was raging. I was busy drawing spirals but my brother Richard was a veritable flea in my ear. He wanted to go down to the Haven as he was certain there would be a wreck that night. I said it was no night to go abroad but Richard wouldn't accept no for an answer. He woke Pa who was slumbering by the fire and there was no arguing with the old bear when it came to following through with something his littlest cub wanted to do. We pulled on our coats and boots and set off into the dreadful night.

The wind was furious. Branches were hurled at us as if by demons. Bits of corrugated iron, ripped from a roof, clattered past as we drove down to the beach.

Earlier in the afternoon the gale had been blowing offshore and we'd joined a group of locals in the Haven to stare at a yacht anchored off shore.

"If that war my boat I wouldn't park it thar," Lloyd remarked, "Come nightfall she'll be blowin onshore and that thar yacht'll be wrecked."

Lloyd was one of three Cowling brothers who farmed up the valley. They were men of the earth, cliffs and woods, the true Cornish of Crackington Haven. Lloyd had long hair, a beard and never wore a shirt and what he didn't know about the sea, weather and local terrain of that part of North Cornwall wasn't worth knowing.

When we reached the beach the wind was blowing onshore and had freshened from gale to storm force. Richard wanted to see if the yacht was wrecked. We went with him down on the shingle where a group was standing and were told, above the screaming wind, that the yacht was abandoned. Apparently it was on transit from Milford Haven to Guernsey and the engine had failed. Two charter men had anchored her in the Haven for shelter but as the wind turned they had been advised by the Coastguard to abandon her and make for the beach in their life raft. They were now washed up in the bar of the Coombe Barton Hotel.

Richard was ecstatic. He had been right all along. The abandoned yacht was sure to be wrecked somewhere on the reef of rocks that surrounded the Haven like the jaws of a shark. All sorts of stuff would be thrown up on the shore but he said we had to get to it before the Cowlings, who usually had the jetsam stowed in their barns before any of us knew there'd even been a wreck. For once I agreed with my kid brother. This time we had be the first to reach the wreck.

As there was no sign of anything in the Haven we reckoned the yacht would be smashed on the Tremoutha reef just south of Crackington. The tide was out so Richard and I ran down to the beach to see if we could get round over the rocks but seething surf from the high seas blocked our passage. When we returned to the Haven, Pa suggested we go home and forget about it.

Richard was downcast. At just thirteen, he still had to do as he was told and go to bed. I had no intention of leaving that wreck for the Cowlings and leaping back into Ma's blue finned Ford Zodiac I flew out of the valley. Roger and my sister Mary were just settling down for the night when I burst into their cottage with the news.

I was certain I could reach the wreck by a cliff-path but I didn't want to go alone. Initially Roger wasn't keen on the idea but after a while he caved into my enthusiasm and agreed we had to beat the Cowlings. So dressing quickly and buckling on his scout knife, he grabbed a flagon of cider and followed me into the storm.

We coasted into the Haven, with the motor off, so as not to attract attention and settled down with the booze to wait for the bar to close and lights in the hamlet to go out. When all was quiet we drove up the coast road to the top of the cliff above Tremoutha Bay.

It was nearly midnight when we set out across the fields into the teeth of the Atlantic storm. We couldn't stand against the tempest. Crawling on hands and knees to the cliff edge we found the path and slipped and slithered down toward the rocky beach. Drenched by sheeting rain and covered in mud we eventually came to the last corner before the perilous path dropped to the shore.

Roger was ahead of me. As I slid the last stretch I bumped into him. He had frozen. Around the bend a hulk leered out of the gloom. Like a stranded whale the yacht was perched on the beach right in front of us. In the wild night it was an eerie sight.

When we recovered from the initial shock, whooping with delight, we leapt down to the shingle and danced round the vessel like a couple of hobgoblins, shrieking and laughing at our amazing good fortune. We were expecting to salvage some bits and pieces from a wreck and instead we found an intact yacht. She must have been blown through a gap in the reef or perhaps the seas were so high they had lifted her above the jagged rocks and deposited her dry on the beach.

We clambered aboard and were astounded at the sight of all the gear. Roger pulled out his knife and hacked at the radio. I found a screwdriver and had the compass dismantled in a jiffy. Within a short while there was a pile of booty on the floor of the wheelhouse, as much as could be carried up the cliff.

I found an empty kitbag. Roger rummaged through the clothing and came out with a leather jacket, a fistful of bank notes and a white seaman's jumper. The kitbag and jumper we stuffed full of loot, shared the cash, and split.

It was good to have some cash in pocket and Roger was delighted with his new leather jacket. The Cowlings would be green with envy.

Swag over shoulders, we commenced our ascent. Struggling ahead of me on the slippery cliff path Roger suddenly turned and hissed out of the inky blackness, "David are you sure we aren't on our first job?"

"Of course not Roger," I replied, "We've just been collecting flotsam and jetsam off the beach!"

We continued the upward sodden scramble in silence. Roger was not convinced.

Sometime around 2:30 a.m. two bedraggled sea urchins burst in on Ma and Pa. Switching on the bedroom lights we emptied our prize onto the floor.

Ma blinked at us, not knowing if she was awake or in the middle of a nightmare. Pa just stared dumbfounded.

Bubbling with boyish excitement, we babbled our story. Covered her face in her hands Ma began to cry, "They've been looting!"

Pa, aware of the seriousness of the situation, grabbed the phone and rang the 24-hour coast-guard service. He announced that a vessel had been abandoned on the high sea and he had taken possession of it for salvage.

He was given the home number the Receiver of Wrecks at Padstow. The next call woke the man from sleep and the claim was staked. The Receiver promised to come up to Crackington Haven in the morning. Pa then rang the Press Agency in Fleet Street:

"My name is Dr Ash and I am ringing to tell you I have taken possession of yacht for salvage....

"Yes for salvage, it has been washed up at Crackington Haven in Cornwall...

"Near Bude, up on the North Coast and I'm claiming wrecker's rights...

"That's right, wrecker's rights...

"What do you mean there is no such thing as wrecker's rights. Here in Cornwall there is! It's tradition. The Cornish always seize wrecks that blow up on the shore."

Pa slammed down the phone. Convinced he had a rightful claim; he got up and told me we were returning to the wreck. Richard was already up and dressed. Roger collapsed on the sofa and was lost to sleep. Pa grabbed a rope and for some reason I picked up an axe.

We scrambled back down the cliff path. It must have been about 4:00 a.m. The storm had passed and all was still. When we reached the yacht Pa immediately secured it to rocks at the base of the cliff with his rope.

"What are you doing?" I exclaimed, "She isn't going to float away from here!"

"That's not the point," retorted Pa, "In order to claim salvage we have to secure the vessel"

With his torch, Richard had discovered the name of our new acquisition.

"Pa," he shouted "She's called the Casketta."

The lad was already up on deck. I scrambled up after him and together we heaved Pa aboard.

Richard disappeared below to explore and Pa and I sat up on deck to discuss a plan of action. It was then I remembered my dream.

Several months earlier I had a dream in which I saw a sailing dingy stranded on the Tremoutha beach with its sails up and flapping in the wind. I wanted to seize it but Stephen talked me out of doing so. Then I met two men coming up the Crackington beach laden with gear from the boat. They had gone along after me and taken possession of the craft. Even in my dream I wondered why they had so much stuff from a dingy and I regretted not taking it myself. I had woken up with bitter disappointment.

It was amazing how I had seen the stranded sailing craft in the precise spot where the Casketta was now beached. It was clear to both Pa and me that my dream was a warning - it was not the first time I had a prophetic dream. But what did it mean? Pa decided to interpret the dream. He said if we relinquished our hold on the wreck we would suffer a disappointment and regret it later. He said whatever the odds we had to stick to our claim. My orders were to stay on the boat and under no circumstances to let anyone else on board.

At the crack of dawn Roger arrived with bacon and eggs from Ma's fridge to cook in the galley. After Pa and Richard had enjoyed a hearty breakfast they left for home. It was about 7:00 a.m. Jolly Roger and I were playing buccaneers in the rigging, when we spotted a solitary figure wending his way down the cliff path. It was a freelance press photographer.

My brother-in-law and I were only too happy to have our picture taken for the papers. Noddy turned pirate picked up his axe for the shot. The photographer was delighted and asked for the axe to be tilted until the blade was clear for the picture. Once I picked up that axe I didn't put it down again.

At about 7:30, two men came round from the Haven. I recognised them. They were the men from my dream! They said that they were the charter men and asked if they could come on board. Brandishing the axe I said no. Deciding not to argue with an axman they retreated to the Haven. Half and hour later they returned with a policeman, and Phil Freestone, the voluntary coastguard and owner of the Coombe Barton Hotel in the Haven. Phil Flintstone, as we called him, had an ongoing feud with Pa.

The policeman came up and glaring at me with cold blue eyes told us to stop fooling about and let the men on board. My 'goody' instinct was to do what the policeman said but remembering my dream and Pa's admonition I held fast and brandishing my axe at him I barked I wasn't letting anyone on board. At the sight of the axe the policeman backed off and joined the others. They were livid and Phil began to shout at me to stand down and let the rightful owners on board.

I was beginning to weaken in my resolve when Pa arrived down the cliff path with reinforcements, including Lloyd Cowling and Liz and Lee Cummins. Pa was dressed in his naval uniform, complete with cane and to further inflame the party of officials he strutted around the yacht, tapping the hull with his stick, bellowing "What a fine vessel I have here."

Encouraged by his antics I placed my boot on the gunwale and laughing at them, I shook my axe at furious Phil and the stone faced policeman.

It was about 11:00 a.m. when an elderly gentleman in uniform and cane came tottering over the rocks from the Haven. He was the Receiver of Wrecks from Padstow.

Pa, dressed as a naval officer was immediately at his side. The Receiver inspected the hull and our ropes fastening it to the cliff. He approved of what we had done to secure the vessel but stressed his jurisdiction was only for vessels beached below high tide. If it was marooned above high tide then it was a matter for the police – who were now gathering in numbers, itching to get their hands on the axe man.

High tide was expected at about noon so we all stood watching and waiting as the waves slowly lapped up the beach ever closer to the hulk. Suddenly a single wave broke against the yacht and water went gurgling under her. A stream of bubbles broke on the beach above. Bubbles saved Noddy that day. He could have been locked away for looting and threatening Plod with an axe; serious offences even in Toy town. But Noddy wasn't done yet!

A cheer went up from the Ash camp. The Freestone party was vanquished. With the authority vested in him by the Crown, the Receiver declared to the assembly that he accepted Dr Ash's claim for salvage. Acknowledging we had made the vessel secure, he instructed that we were to remove and store in a place of safety whatever we could take from it and allow the charter men to collect their personal belongings from the store. The police had to leave without felons.

Roger was behind my back hissing for me to empty my pockets of half the haul of cash he'd given me so he could replenish the pockets of the leather jacket he had 'salvaged'.

He then hastened up the cliff path to make sure all the other effects were in order before the rightful owners arrived.

Fortune lost I went for fame. I'd noticed a group of reporters gathered round Pa on the rocks and I swaggered across to them with my axe. The fellow from the *Daily Express* asked me, "Mister Ash, if the policeman had tried to board the yacht would you have used the axe on him?"

Noddy closed his eyes and deliberated for a moment. Should he say *yes* or should he say *no?* It was playtime and he wasn't playing monk anymore; he was playing brigand so he replied with an emphatic, "Yes."

Reporters scribbled in scruffy notebooks. The following morning headlines in the national dailies read, 'Axe Brandishing Maniac Threatens Police'. Never believe what you read in the papers. They reported Dr Ash as the axe brandishing maniac. The fellow who photographed me with the axe told he sold the picture to the *Daily Telegraph* for £400. My ego was peeved that readers were told the maniac in the picture as Pa rather than me.

As the Haven hit the headlines an impromptu meeting of incensed residents was held at the Coombe Barton. Radicals, led by an Australian called Chris, pressed for a hanging from the rigging but the conservatives, led by Mike Preller won the day in favour of economic sanctions.

All Ashes were banned, forthwith, from the pub, cafes and most of the local shops. Chris owned the local petrol station. He threatened to shoot any one of us who so much as dared to venture onto his forecourt.

The charter men returned to Milford Haven and Ma took to her bed with flu. As for the rest of us, we had possession of the craft but didn't know what to do with it. Casketta was stuck fast on the beach waiting for the next storm to smash her up.

There was nothing for it but to sit tight and wait on fortune. Pa, with the indomitable faith of his Jewish ancestors, sat in silence anticipating a sign from heaven.

Mr. Primrose, from the marine insurance company was the first to break the monotony of days. In the Coombe Barton he had boasted that he could sort out the Ashes but he hadn't reckoned on the stubbornness of Pa. He spent hours arguing but got nowhere. Pa insisted that the yacht was his for salvage and there was nothing more to be said.

On the third brooding day Nick Robinson suddenly interrupted a dull afternoon. Nick was a student of law. His mum lived just up from the Haven. Determined not to miss the fun he had driven down from London with a bevy of barristers and a pile of legal tomes. Nick had convinced his buddies from the bar we had a claim worth thousands.

Within an hour of their arrival, there was another knock at the door. This time it was John England of Padstow. John, the owner of a marine salvage business had come up from Padstow unannounced. The evening before, while he was having his tea, he had watched a programme on television where an expert discussing our claim had said that if we could get the yacht off the beach it was worth £3,000 in salvage. Nick had seen the same programme.

John England was the only person in North Cornwall with the equipment and know-how to get the Casketta off the beach and he knew it. He wanted to buy our claim and being Cornish he would have offered paltry sum but he hadn't reckoned on Nick and his bank of barristers. They pounced on him and after some wrangling secured an offer of £1,000.

Pa and I did nothing but watch the choreography of the gods. We accepted the offer and sold our rights to the wreck. The lawyers drafted a contract which John signed. He said work would start the following day in the hope of catching the evening high tide. The spring tides were waning and if the attempt failed it could be another month before there would be sufficient water to float her off.

When John England left there was jubilation in the house. The only dark cloud on the horizon was the weather outlook. Another storm was forecast but Pa was unperturbed. "Calm as a mill-pond," he kept saying, "It will be as calm as a mill-pond."

The following morning was bright and sunny. John England and his salvage team were on Tremoutha beach early, making the hull watertight with fiberglass patches.

Nick Robinson and his chums had arrived ahead of us and collected the money from John, £500 in cash and a £500 cheque. Nick suggested that one of us drive down to Padstow immediately to cash the cheque.

With a roar of the engine and skidding tires Roger was off in the Zodiac to Padstow but first he dropped Pa off to nurse Ma with the banknotes. As soon as she saw the cash she made a miraculous recovery.

I scrambled down the cliff and joined the other able bodied men who gathered on the shore to help manhandle the vessel as far down the beach as possible. The Cowling brothers were there. It was still a mystery how they had missed the Casketta. Nothing was said; they just heaved and pushed the hull over greased planks with the rest of us.

The afternoon air was still and the sea as calm as a millpond. At about 3:00 John's coastal steamer arrived from Padstow and sailed into Tremoutha Bay. A line was fastened to the Casketta and as the tide slowly edged its way up and under her, the steamer pulled and we pushed with might and main. At about 4:00 p.m., when the tide was full, the Casketta suddenly lurched and slid and then bobbing momentarily in the water, she leapt to the line from her tug as a puppy yanked on its lead. John England was already on board as the yacht moved out to sea. A cheer went up from the beach and from the cliff tops, lined with spectators and a television team. People were waving in the festive atmosphere.

I ran back up the cliff path to watch her go. It was an unforgettable sight. Under a cloudless sky on a sea like silk, the Casketta rounded the headland of Cam Beak, out of sight and out of our lives.

Later, when I was chatting with Lloyd I asked him why he hadn't bothered with the Casketta. He told me he and his brothers had been busy with another wreck up the coast at Cleave. A solitary sad seaman had been saved but his vessel was smashed in the storm. No one knew about that wreck. There was no mention, even in the local paper.

Pa, Roger and I had £300 each and Richard £100 for initiating the venture. Ma spent his money on school fees. Apparently he mentioned something about a new bike but his plea went unheard!

Stephen returned home early from his holiday in France. He was ropeable. He had picked up the news of our antics when he spotted a picture of me with my axe in a French newspaper. Fortunately I was able to pay him his £100. I didn't mention the car.

First came money, then came a woman. Roger introduced me to his cousin, Penny who fancied a pirate. She happened to be baby-sitting Chris's kids and wasted no time in inviting me over to his place for an evening.

Noddy pulled up on the forbidden forecourt with the car engine running, expecting to flee the barrel of a shotgun. Penny came out laughing to say the coast was clear. Chris and his wife had just left and they weren't due back until the following morning!

We spent the evening in front of the television until Penny said it was time for bed. Still in monkish mode I got up to leave but she whispered in my ear, "Chris said he would shoot you if you even came on his fore-court; come on lets desecrate his bed!"

My hymn had been heard in heaven, my prayer in the monastery answered and I was confident my Carmelite confessors would have agreed that the greater sin would have been to throw aside such an opportunity! The following morning found me in Chris' bed, my smug smile of sweet satisfaction enhanced by a dish of bacon and eggs from Chris' fridge, fried by Penny with his gas on his stove. Leaping into my Triumph, I drove off triumphant from his forbidden forecourt into Bude where I bought a brand new Olivetti portable electric typewriter.

Chapter 16
Creative Evolution

Pa's eyes see beauty and are beauty because beauty shines within.

Steven Ash

In October 1973 I commenced a one-year post graduate course at the College of St Mark and St John that had moved to the edge of Dartmoor near Plymouth. With my B.Sc. degree from London University, I decided to teach physics. The college was in the midst of transfer to Devon from London. Stephen was in his third year and it was great to be with him and I enjoyed the freedom in the college allowed by the chaos of change.

Left to my own devices, apart from teaching practice and a few lectures, I had ample time to devote to my physics. My new electric typewriter was fantastic as it enabled me to write as quickly as ideas popped into my head. I wrote and re-wrote papers to clarify my thinking. Also my car gave me access to Dartmoor where my spirit could soar. The college had an excellent library and the physics teaching course kept me in touch with the subject and fortuitously I was sponsored into the Royal Institution by a student I befriended called Donalda.

The music also moved forward as Steven and I found an ally in the audio visual aids department in the form of Neil Tugwell. Neil provided us with a recording studio and sound engineering so that we could record an album of our songs. Jenny, Simon and Richard came down to Plymouth and joined us for the recordings.

Preparing for a career in physics my innovative thinking transferred to biology. As a trainee science teacher I felt a need to reconcile my Catholic faith in Creation with my scientific belief in Darwin's theory of evolution. I pondered on the issue until I had a resolution to the seemingly intractable dichotomy.

My premise was; if particles of energy were particles of pure movement and were more like thoughts than things, then the Universe would be a mind and obviously intelligence would underlie everything - including evolution.

When I was at Queens studying zoology we were taught that parasites were very smart. The larva of a parasite that infected cattle was cited. At one stage in its complex life cycle it entered the head of an ant and caused it to climb a blade of grass and clamp its jaws on the blade. Browsing cattle would then eat the grass, swallow the infected ant and become infected themselves. No scientist could ever convince me there wasn't intelligence underlying that. The larva might not do math or speak French but then it didn't need that sort of intelligence to get a cow to swallow it.

But the Christian idea of God the Creator being only good with life all figured out before life happened didn't square with me. I realised that God - as depicted in the Bible – could not be both good and the Creator at the same time.

The reason again was parasites. At Queens I was fascinated by parasites. Why would a good God deliberately create little creatures that make other creatures sick and miserable? Flat worms or flukes are a type of parasite that plague all things that live. Liver fluke and tape worms, itchy bottom nematode worms and the diabolical fork tailed flukes that cause bilharzias or elephantitis are examples of this devilish breed. A God that created those nasty things would be malicious and cruel - the devil himself - anything but good.

It made more sense to me that if God were the intelligence underlying life, God would be creating by trial and error. I called that process 'creative evolution'. I saw no reason why evolution should not be the means through which God developed the multitude of life forms that populate our world. It even struck me that God could be evolving through life! Maybe God was learning and growing by breaking things down and then building them up again better than before.

In zoology I had been taught that the flat worms were the earliest type of worm. They weren't deliberately nasty it's just they had a problem; a fundamental design fault. The peristalsis – waves of muscle contraction – that moved them toward their food also pushed food out of their gut. They couldn't both move and eat so they found a way to thwart the ruthless execution of natural selection by residing in other creatures bodies. There they could eat without moving. They became parasites preying on all other species to survive.

Mark two model 'segmented worms', earthworms, lugworms and suchlike, then appeared on the scene with a split between the muscles around their guts and under their skin. The split separated the waves of muscle contraction moving food through the gut from the muscles working for locomotion. This was one of the greatest developments in the 'creative evolution' of life on earth. All more advanced animals, us included, are developments of the segmented worm. We all have the split between our gut muscles and our other body muscles with vital organs hanging in between and the segments of bone in our spine are a development of this worm's segmentation. Here was a prime example of intelligence learning from mistakes. The faults in an early model became apparent and improvements were made to overcome them. To me this was obviously intelligence at work operating through 'creative evolution'.

The Bible story of creation without evolution appeared to be a myth but so was the science teaching that evolution was based on lucky flukes. The speculation that evolutionary genetic changes were pure blind chance seemed as stupid as faith in God bringing all birds and animals into instant perfect existence like some fairy godmother waving her magic wand!

The neo-Darwinian idea of unintelligent evolution (represented today by Richard Dawkins who is vehemently anti-God) completely missed the mark to my mind. The extraordinary diversity and dazzling beauty of life screamed 'intelligence' at me. Once I realised God hadn't cracked it to begin with but was operating a system of trial and error, then far from seeing evolution in conflict with God, I believed that through his theory of evolution Darwin was making a major contribution to our understanding of God.

I was of the opinion Darwin's greatest masterpiece was the idea of natural selection. That made sense to me because a process of selection is necessary in every system of production. I could see how selection revealed mistakes in my work. I could not see the errors myself. I relied on others to spot the flaws. I would subsequently solve the problems and move on. I was confident God used natural selection to reveal mistakes in creation and grew in wisdom therefrom.

I experienced problems as a gift. Only when I was confronted with a problem in physics did a solution pop into my mind. Criticism pruned dead wood from my work and mauled my brain-babies akin to natural selection on the Savannah. Invariably better ones would take their place.

I needed a decent typewriter to write out my ideas in physics so I could get students and scientists to read them. I had used this process for years to gather criticism. More often than not the scientists shredded my work. I would go away disheartened until a solution appeared. Dejection would then turn to delight and I would rewrite my ideas all over again and repeat the process. That to me was the process of creative evolution at work; building something up, watching it perform then breaking it down to reconstruct in a better way. That was the eternal cycle of creation, preservation and destruction – birth, life, death and then rebirth. I couldn't see how God could create in any other way. It took the genius of Darwin to see the detail of how God did what was merely glossed over in the Bible.

In my personal process of evolution, intelligence was at work. Not just in my head, because most solutions didn't come from my thinking, but through my head. My best ideas came to me. I would think and think and think until I was exhausted and eventually give up thinking then suddenly a good idea would pop into my mind.

Breakthroughs often came first thing in the morning as I woke up. In brainstorming sessions, I would often get major inspirations. I was confident the same process was at work through evolution. Inspiration from dimensions beyond the speed of light could have influenced the genetic changes behind the evolutionary process. 'Why not,' I argued, 'If our world is part of the worlds formed of greater speeds of light, then intelligent beings in those worlds could influence evolutionary events in our world.'

It was my rationale for angels all over again. Were angels the agents of intelligent evolution? The Bible suggested they were! In Genesis where the knife held hand of Abraham was stayed by an angel, the angel spoke as God. But I was losing faith in the Bible. If the Bible was unclear whether God was angel or creator of the Universe it wasn't really a solid basis for debating evolution or anything else.

Nonetheless I believed angels were influencing the evolution of my life. Often in a stream of writing or speaking I would experience inspiration. It felt as though I was receiving information. In my life and in my work I was witness to a greater intelligence than my own mind at work from behind the scenes. Beyond my ego and well-planned arrangements, I was fed solutions to problems. There were powers protecting me in my follies and providing for my needs in unexpected and often outrageous ways. I was so protected. I often thought about the single wave breaking under the Casketta that saved me from the police. I didn't know what the intelligence was or where it came from. The only thing I knew for certain was that whatever or whoever was caring for me and guiding me had a wicked sense of humour. Something or someone was setting me up in comic situations and what better opportunity for fun than at my very first meeting with prospective parents-in-law!

Chapter 17
A Party at the Royal Institution

"The best way to survive marriage is to be hopeless and helpless!"

Michael Ash

It was the summer of 1974. Stephen and I were working on a new song in the open plan living room of our new home in Cornwall. The evening light, dancing in the treetops, was slanting through the windows that reached into the roofline. Ma was at the sink looking out across the stream, running as a torrent in that wet July. Suddenly she turned from her dishes and shouted across to me, "David you are going to meet your Waterloo!"

"What?"

"You are going to get married."

"What, to Loretta?"

I'd met Loretta in London and we had just started dating. I sensed she was looking for a husband so it didn't come as a shock to me to be warned of marriage.

"No it won't be Loretta. It will be someone you haven't met yet and she will sweep you off your feet." Ma replied emphatically, drying her hands on a tea towel.

I was in shock.

"You're not serious Ma?"

In my heart I knew she was right. Stephen and I were about to start teaching in London and I was looking forward to some fun. I didn't feel ready to settle; but then does any young man?

"But you won't get married immediately," my mother comforted me. For once she was wrong!

At the beginning of September, Stephen and I moved into the old college of St Mark and St John on the Kings Rd., Chelsea. It had been converted into a teacher's hostel. On my first day there I met a girl but our liaison was short lived. I think I was a bit hasty. She didn't take kindly to my suggestion we skip formalities and go straight to bed.

On the second day I was determined to meet someone but to no avail. By teatime I was getting desperate. At dinner, with tray in hand, I looked round the canteen for an empty seat by a girl but all were occupied.

The only vacant chair in the room was opposite a bloke! I slammed my tray on the table and glowered at him. The poor fellow hurriedly swallowed his pudding and left. I sat down, stuffed a sausage into my mouth and glanced up.

A tall blonde girl with a tray of food was sailing gracefully in my direction. Pointing to the recently emptied position in front of me, I then stabbed determinedly with my finger for her to sit down. With a surprised look on her face she did just that.

She was so lovely I nearly choked on my supper. Unable to chew or swallow I just sat for a few moments, in silence looking into her face. I knew immediately I had just met my wife.

She broke the silence introducing herself as Anna.

Later, Anna told me her immediate opinion of me was that I was a prick out of public school. When I found my tongue and started a breathless run-down on my life story she realised she was wrong about the public school.

I told her all about Pa's inventions, and my unsuccessful attempt, the previous year, to enter a Carmelite monastery before she got through her cabbage. The swing from monk to axe-brandishing maniac took her to the apple pie and custard.

Before I launched into quantum physics Anna managed to squeeze in an invite to her room for a coffee. Toward midnight I had finished my frenzied dissertation. As I left her room I thought I'd blown my chances but I hadn't.

Three days later, sitting in a bath, Anna decided I was the man she would marry. But by then I was out of my bath and getting cold feet - I think most men do when confronted with Waterloo – and was thinking more of a brother-sister relationship.

A couple of evenings after we met I was in Anna's room and forgetting she was only supposed to be a sister, suggested we slip under the duvet for a cuddle. Anna was apprehensive but agreed on condition we kept our underwear on. I leapt into her bed and she slipped in after.

"You've got nothing on!" Anna's voice was up a decibel.

"So will you in a minute," I laughed.

She put up a fight but I was stronger. Her bra was off and on the floor in a jiffy and I had her panties down to her knees when there was a sudden knock on the door. Thinking it was Steven I poked my head out from under the duvet and shouted, "Go away".

There was silence for a moment then a women's voice, rang out loud and clear, "You'll never guess who it is!"

Anna guessed immediately. She could have called out, 'Wait a minute while I catch my pet mouse' or 'Hang on a sec, I've just spilt my coffee' but she did neither. Instead she exploded off the bed, pulled on a dressing gown, switched on the lights and flung open the door.

Naked and bewildered I was left to my own devices. I found my shirt but not my underpants. I was shrinking fast but not fast enough and in the mayhem I was standing, the full Monty at half-mast, facing the open door. It framed a tall gentleman and his wife dressed for the opera. They were up to town and wanted to give their daughter a surprise outing to Covent Garden. I found my trousers but in the rush the zip got stuck fast on the pubic hairs. Anna introduced me to her mother and father. She then threw the duvet back on the bed and her dad, stepping over her bra and my missing underpants, settled into the armchair in the corner. Anna's mum planted herself on the bed. We proceeded to small talk.

Anna and I visited her parents at their country house in Surrey the following weekend. I asked her father for his daughter's hand in marriage. Under the circumstances Bonny had to admit defeat at Waterloo!

On one of our visits I shared my vortex ideas with Anna's dad. Leaning on a spade he looked at me quizzically for a moment and suggested the quantum vortex was a system of increasingly compact lines of force.

That was typical of Cdr. John Bingham, RN, OBE. He would take an encounter with the garden a spade and transform it into an epoch making moment. His description of the vortex as increasingly compact lines of force inspired me to fit my model with the lines of force described by Michael Faraday at the Royal Institution.

Two years previously my father had taken me into the Royal Institution in Albemarle Street near Piccadilly, to show me where Michael Faraday had made his major discoveries. We spent a while under the marble statue on the staircase leading up to the historic Victorian lecture theatre then as we peered into the auditorium Pa turned to me and declared, "David, this is where your work will be launched."

At the first meeting I attended as a young member I was invited onto the Young Members committee and given the task to find suitable lecturers for the monthly meetings. I offered myself. The chairman of the committee, a longhaired university student, was interested in my ideas and suggested Wednesday, January 15th, 1975.

The date posed a problem. The ground floor lecture theatre, normally used by the Young Members, was already booked for another event. It was suggested I give my talk in a room usually used as a cloakroom. I wasn't having that. No way was I going to launch my life work from a loo! Despite reassurances there were no urinals, only coat rails that would be removed for my talk, I would not settle for that room. I was told that the main lecture theatre was free that evening and there was nothing in the rules that said it could not be used by the Young Members but it was a question of numbers. At least a hundred people would be required to warrant its use. Despite the fact the Young Members Group had never met there before I was determined to speak from the historic rostrum of Michael Faraday in the main amphitheatre, as predicted by my father, so I devised a plan.

We were allowed to invite guests to the lectures so I sent out formal invitations to everyone I knew including my family and friends and our colleagues in the schools. Within a fortnight I had a guest list of over a hundred. Going back to the secretary of the Royal Institution I asked how we were to fit more than a hundred people into the cloakroom. She said that was obviously impossible so she let us have the main lecture theatre, famous for the BBC TV Christmas Lectures for my evening.

I was jubilant. Lord Kelvin had demonstrated his vortex theory for the atom with smoke boxes in that historic place. Other great names in Victorian science had spoken there, including, James Clerk Maxwell, Charles Darwin, and Lord Rutherford. I was going to speak from the very rostrum from where the concept of lines of force had been first presented to the world by Michael Faraday.

The great day finally arrived. I had prepared a slide show and hired evening dress for the occasion. Everyone I'd invited came including my parents and grandmother, my uncles and aunts, cousins, brothers, sisters and most of my friends, and Steven's. Loretta turned up with her fiancé and my old flame Diana, They brought as many friends as they could find. Even Pa's long lost brother, Bob arrived. We hadn't seen him for years nor his other brother Jock who turned up too with all my cousins on his side of the family. Peter's fairy godmother, auntie Betty arrived from Tunbridge Wells and most of Anna's family and friends came along with as many teachers as we could muster from the schools where we were teaching.

The guest of honour was the Apostolic Delegate, Archbishop Heim, rustled up by Ma's sister Denise. He sat beside Pa on one of the thrones at the front reserved for Royalty and such like. That was how Pa got to meet the Pope's ambassador in London.

The Young Members arrived in jeans and sweatshirts and were out of place in the great auditorium full of folk in full evening dress. I didn't dare tell them the evening was formal in case word got back to the director of the Royal Institution. I didn't want my plan to be thwarted.

Anna and I had borrowed sheets from the hostel and trestle tables from her school. We hired glasses and bought sherry, cheese and peanuts. To follow my talk we'd planned a sherry reception for the guests after the custom of the Royal Institution.

It was the grandest night the Young Members ever had. Few people understood my lecture but that didn't matter. The massive columns and great marble staircase, glittering chandeliers and famous amphitheatre, the portraits of the greatest scientists in history said everything. Sherry was sipped and cheese and peanuts nibbled in surroundings as prestigious as London could manage. It was an evening my family and friends would never forget.

Anna made the most of the opportunity to hand out wedding invitations. She saved a fortune in postage!

Ma was really proud of me and my maternal Nana was in tears. Wiping her eyes, she said it was a red-letter day for her; the best family gathering she could recall. She passed away shortly after. It was the last time she saw many of her family members. Cousin Nicholas said I was outrageous throwing a family party at the Royal Institution. He wasn't the only one to view my evening as outrageous. Sir George Porter, director of the Royal Institution was outraged. He came up to me at the following meeting, purple with anger, and hissed, "Don't you ever, ever do that again." .

That's not the sort of party one repeats in a lifetime!

Simon came to the lecture with his new wife Maria and members of her Italian family. He was well into his dentistry course and she was studying physiotherapy. Simon went onto become a consultant in orthodontics with a Fellowship of the Royal College of Surgeons. Simon and Maria reared three beautiful daughters and with the Bishop of London in Maria's family they remained staunch Catholics. Simon never strayed from orthodoxy so Jenny's husband Alan described him as the black sheep of the Ash family 'the only Ash with short hair and a long mortgage'.

Despite being sensible, Simon, more than any of us, continued in Pa's footsteps at the inventor in the family. He developed a revolutionary way of improving the efficiency of running hospital departments by a system of barcodes linking patients to procedures and prescriptions but like his father before him, he met with considerable resistance and inertia from the establishment. He also developed a tiny plate to protect the palates of premature babies from deformity due to inserted tubes. More recently he invented a brace to realign the jaw during sleep to reduce and in many cases, eliminate snoring. For that I think he deserves the Nobel Peace Prize!

Chapter 18
Fawlty Teacher

"David, you should get John Cleese to act out your life."

Michael Ash

At the time of my lecture at the Royal Institution I was a science teacher in a London Catholic school in Maida Vale. I had a class of thirteen and fourteen year olds but I was at a loss to understand why they suddenly started calling me 'Basil'. Why were groups giggling at me when I crossed the playground or passed them in the corridors? It was 1975. I had started an evening MSc course in nuclear and particle physics at Birkbeck College so I was too busy to watch television. I had no idea *Fawlty Towers* had started on the BBC. People say I am the splitting image of John Cleese and the kids at school were quick to notice my resemblance in looks and behaviour to Basil Fawlty!

Trouble began for Basil when a new head of department was appointed. He was an ex-marine sergeant who had taken his post at the same time as I took mine. His predecessor had appointed us both then left us to it. The disciplinarian took an instant dislike to me. I was constantly reminded that I would never have been taken on if he'd had a say in the matter.

The bad chemistry went exothermic when I took my class on a demonstration to Parliament. It was the days before Greenpeace and after listening to a song about the Blue whale by Gordon Lightfoot I felt desperate for the plight of the whales and I shared my concern with my pupils. They picked up on the emotion and agreed it was time to take direct action. We would lobby Parliament to stop the bloody slaughter!

Surprisingly the headmaster was in support of our idea so we spent a couple of weeks painting 'Save the Whale' banners, gathering signatures on a petition and collecting letters of permission from parents. Everything was going according to plan until we came to board the bus to Westminster.

Two buses arrived at the same time and most of the gang clambered aboard the wrong one and headed off to Trafalgar Square. On arrival at the Palace of Westminster in the right bus I had only ten pupils with me. A television film crew, that had arrived to film us for the ITV children's programme, *Magpie*, wondered why there were so few children. It was all very embarrassing. I had to apologise for losing two thirds of my class. I knew they were somewhere in London but I couldn't say where!

The Liberal M.P., Paddy Ashdown came out to receive our petition and seemed pleased to see us despite the poor turnout. Then suddenly the police arrived.

"Does this lot belong to you?" called the voice of authority. "We found them marching with banners down Whitehall."

The pupils flanked by police identified me as their teacher. The stern police sergeant continued, "Did you know they were breaking the law marching down Whitehall?"

Paddy Ashdown and the film crew from Magpie smiled and pretended not to notice.

"Seeing as they are only kids," continued the policeman, with the long look of the law, "We'll let you get away with it this time. But don't do it again!"

Judging from their rosy faces and sparkling eyes, the mob of kids who had just done a march down Whitehall were none the worse for being on the wrong side of the law.

"Cor sir, you should have been with us, we had a great demo," shouted one of the fourteen year-olds.

"Hey Bas, we chanted 'save the whales' all the way from Trafalgar Square," exclaimed another enthusiastic young protester.

It was fortunate I wasn't with them. Only a group of unaccompanied children could get away with an unlawful demonstration past Downing Street! They did their march and made their statement for the future of their world. With the number of police surrounding them on their march there is no way they could have either got lost or come to any harm.

The next day a double page spread on the plight of the whales appeared in the middle of the *Daily Mirror* and an article reported the march. That same evening the kids were stoked to see themselves on the Magpie television programme which was devoted entirely to the desperate predicament of the whales.

My class got their message for the welfare of the environment out to children throughout the country. It was a good lesson for them to make a statement and take direct action and empowering for them to help bring about change for the better. I am sure it was coincidence but I still like to think they initiated the 'Save the Whale' movement that came to the fore around that time.

Members of staff were divided in their opinion of my extra-curricular lesson. Some thought the demonstration was a good exercise but others gave it a black mark. The staff room buzzed like a hornet nest. I decided to skip coffee.

However, it wasn't my class outing to Westminster that turned sniping from my staff sergeant into an artillery barrage. It was the trip I organised to Watford!

Most members of my class were ardent fans of the Watford football team. When they heard I had never even been to a football match, let alone seen Watford play, they were shocked. They kept pestering me to go along with them to see their favourite team play at home and they wouldn't accept 'no' for an answer.

Against my better judgment I agreed to go to Watford for the next home match. I arranged with the parents to take three boys and a girl after school and decided not to mention anything to the headmaster, my head of department or other members of staff.

A lad called Plummer wanted to come too but the others gave an emphatic no. I couldn't understand why. Plummer was a nice kid. He sat at the back of the class, did his lessons and was never any trouble.

"Don't take Plummer sir, what ever you do, don't take Plummer," they warned.

I felt sad as I liked the lad but I was outclassed so Plummer got left behind.

The fateful day arrived and after school the fortunate four tumbled into the back of my black Morris Minor van and we headed north.

Watford was on top form and I was just getting into the match when Plummer turned up. The kid had a half bottle of Teachers whisky upturned to his lips. My immediate thought was 'what an appropriate brand name'. He offered me a sip but I declined.

The favoured four told him to leave but I thought they were being mean so I invited him to stay. "Plummer is part of our class," I lectured, switching on my teacher's voice. Unfortunately I forgot one of the most important lessons for teacher is to listen to your class. Stupidly, I not only invited Plummer to join us, I offered him a lift home!

"You'll regret it sir!" said the girl, confiscating what was left of the whisky.

We left the grounds with Plummer reeling after us. Then, to my abject horror the little vandal pulled out of his pocket a small pot of black enamel paint. Flicking off the lid he proceeded to pour it all over the windscreen and bonnet of a brand new white Ghia Ford Granada.

"Run," I shrieked and bolted with the rest of the kids. They kicked Plummer as they pushed him into the back of the van before scrambling aboard. With a scream of tires we left Watford. Driving was difficult because periodically Plummer would stick his leg into the back of my head.

Half-way down the Kilburn High road there was a cry from the back, "Quick, Mr. Ash, stop, Plummer's going to be sick!"

I shot into a side street, slammed on the brakes and leapt out to open the back doors. Plummer fell at my feet, rolled down the road and threw-up in the gutter. I didn't know what to do with him. How could I, as a responsible teacher, deliver a drunk kid back to his parents?

Basil had to think fast and he had a brain wave. He heaved the yob back in the van and sped on up the hill. Suddenly he spotted a churchyard surrounded by a low wall. Just what he was looking for; he pulled over and shouted, "All out!"

The incapacitated Plummer was dragged out of the van and onto the pavement. Basil took hold of his wrists and instructed the others to grab his ankles. The boy was then lifted into the air and Basil began to swing him to the count of, "One......two....."

Fortunately, there was a girl in the party. She dropped Plummer's foot and demanded, "Sir what are we doing?"

"We're going to chuck Plummer over this wall and leave him to sober up in the bushes then he can find his own way home," Basil replied, "Now come on, grab his leg."

A howl of protest went up. Basil was the only one left holding a limb. His class had mutinied.

"Sir, we can't do that!"

"He'll die of exposure!"

"But I can't take him home in this state," Basil objected, "His parents will murder me."

"Leave that to us," the class chorused confidently.

Basil was out voted and over ruled.

Plummer was heaved back into the van while Basil settled disconsolate behind the wheel. He drove to Plummer's place and waited outside while the kids carried their incapacitated compatriot upstairs.

After a short while, Basil was invited into the flat. Plummer's mum and dad proffered coffee and biscuits. His team-mates smiled at him over rims of hot chocolate. As the Fawlty teacher settled on the sofa Mr. and Mrs. Plummer said how much their boy liked his lessons and they were very grateful he had been brought him home safe, if not sound.

Next day Plumber turned up in class bruised from the thrashing his dad gave him but otherwise he was in good spirits. I got the cat-o-nine-tongues from my head of department. He said it was unheard of for a teacher to take pupils to a football match even out of school hours. Fortunately he never heard half of the caper with Plummer!

After that outing I had difficulty in maintaining class discipline. I had crossed the line. Every lesson turned into a football match! One kid in particular was a right little hooligan. Toward the end of a chemistry lesson I lost my temper and gave the nasty little Manuel a Basil smack on the head. At the moment of impact he happened to be balancing on one leg of his stool pulling faces at a friend. My clip about the ear caused him to lose his balance. As he fell his chin caught the edge of the lab bench.

I was called to the headmaster's office.

"What did you do to that boy?"

"I smacked him on the head, sir."

"And then what happened?"

"He lost his balance and fell off his stool, sir."

The headmaster didn't speak for a moment. He just sat looking at me.

"He broke his neck!"

"Oh!"

"Did you realise?"

"No sir."

"Did you know he had only one kidney?"

"No sir."

"He is the only child in school with only one kidney."

"Oh!"

Sickness rose in the pit of my stomach. I promised to be a better teacher in future; if there was a future!

"Look, I am on your side," said the headmaster with genuine sympathy. "I appreciate how hard it is for you young teachers to maintain order in the classroom. I know it is easy to lose control. Do you belong to a union?"

"Yes sir."

He mused for a moment, tapping his pen.

"Have you got a solicitor?"

"No sir."

"I suggest you find one!"

The word solicitor stirred the sickness in my stomach. It was a growing nightmare. I couldn't believe it was happening. I glanced around his office wondering where he kept his cane. That would have been so easy. After a sharp pain the whole thing would be over and done with. But the roles had changed and the rules were different.

The headmaster put on his glasses and looked down at the notes on his desk.

He articulated slowly, "This boy's parents are not the sort to make complaints."

After a few moments he looked up at me over the rim of his glasses, "You may be lucky and get away with it otherwise, there is not a lot I can do for you."

I thanked him for his concern. He showed me to the door and shook me firmly by the hand.

"Do you pray?"

"Yes sir."

"I suggest you pray the rosary."

I prayed. Mary and the angels must have heard my plea. The parents accepted the incident as an unfortunate accident and didn't take action. Fortunately it was hairline crack and not a hangman's fracture.

The lad was back in class showing off his neck brace the very next morning. I never had any trouble from him after that. At the end of the lesson he cleaned the blackboard for me and hung around for a chat. Fawlty teacher learnt an important lesson at school that day. The way to win respect of the pupils was to break their necks.

Chapter 19
Exploring Consciousness

"Breathing is the source of healing. As God breathed the breath of life into Adam so remember to breathe the breath of life into every situation of your life."

Michael Ash

I gave a lecture at Surrey University attended by members of the faculty of physics. I remember it well because Ma came with me and sat in the front row. During question time one of the physicists asked for my account for the strong nuclear force. I had none. He replied that while he was impressed with what I had achieved so far, unless or until I could explain the force that held the nucleus of the atom together professional physicists would never take my vortex physics seriously.

I didn't feel animosity toward him. He was sincerely interested in my ideas and pointed me in a direction I needed to take. In response I started the part time course in nuclear and particle physics at Birkbeck College. But once again the Universe had different designs for me. The brakes had been applied to my exploration into physics. I was about to become the father of many children and begin my exploration into consciousness.

Anna and I were married on the 31st March 1975. She was already pregnant with twins. Over the following August we swapped our flat on Prince of Wales Drive in Battersea for the family home in Crackington to enjoy a summer holiday in

Cornwall. Ma and Pa moved into our large and well-appointed flat and Pa set up in practice. All he needed was some patients.

Steven had introduced Pa to an acupuncturist called Gerald Clerk who invited him to meet a group of people who were sure to be interested in his holistic approaches. Gerald first took Pa to meet them in a squat. As he entered a voice inside Pa's head declared, "These are my people!"

Gerald then took Ma and Pa to a disused cinema in Dulwich that had been converted into a meditation centre where they met more of the followers of a boy from India called Guru Maharaji also known as Maharaji and Prem Pal.

Ma was fascinated by the Indian culture and wanted to find out about the young teacher and the Knowledge he was spreading. Pa was more interested in sharing his ideas with the guru's followers who were very receptive to him.

Within a month Ma had been initiated into Maharaji's Knowledge and began to practice meditation. Pa went with her to Dulwich almost every evening to listen to the discourses called 'satsang'. Very quickly his consulting room in our Battersea flat was full of patients. The young people from the center, who called themselves 'premies,' came to him in droves for his natural medicine. Pa was so busy he asked to stay on with us into the autumn. Anna agreed, but only until the babies arrived.

The understanding we had with Pa was that he could use our flat in the day while we were at school but inevitably there was a cross over and often, when we arrived home in the evening our front room was still full of premies waiting their turn to see him. We never minded because usually there was a delicious evening meal ready for us when we arrived home. They called it service. It was part of their spiritual discipline to do things for others.

Initially we were alarmed that Ma and Pa might be joining a cult. We were also concerned that they could lose all their money. However, Pa was making money rather than losing it and there was an undeniable sense of peace about the premies. In the waiting room they didn't talk or read magazines but sat silent with their eyes closed. When I asked them what they were doing they said to me, "We are not waiting, we are meditating!"

I began to listen as they spoke about their young teacher and the gift of Knowledge he had given them. Their words touched my heart. My head was full of doubts but my heart was pulling and the pull was getting stronger.

More than anything else it was the satsang that drew me. I loved the way the premies spoke about the importance of meditation and sharing truth for awakening consciousness. I was delighted to have found a group of people who were receptive to my ideas and what they said concurred with my burgeoning physics of consciousness.

To explore consciousness I needed a guide. Accepting an Indian guru was a challenge to my Catholicism and I was still very attached to Garabandal. However, I was also profoundly impressed by the Yogic Philosophy and reading the 'Autobiography of a Yogi' by Yogananda rekindled my thirst for wisdom from the East. I decided to ask for the Knowledge. It was free. I had nothing to lose.

When I received Knowledge I was taught to direct my attention from thinking to being aware. Meditating on the Knowledge enabled me to explore consciousness, not by thinking about it but by experiencing it as reality.

Meditation became vital for me. The danger with my theoretical physics was it involved a lot of mental activity. Meditation quieted my mind and brought me back into the moment. When I received Knowledge I was shown a center of stillness where I could experience myself as pure consciousness.

I still consider Knowledge the greatest gift I received in this lifetime, surpassing even the knowledge I received through the vortex; as it was just for me. The knowledge of the vortex came from yoga but the Knowledge I received was yoga. It was union with my true self. Through Knowledge I reached real stillness where there was no separation; I became the consciousness I was talking about. It was as though I had been shown my source of awareness as a pool, presenting a reflection of what I truly was. Thoughts were like a breeze that ruffled the surface, obscuring the reflection.

Through the practice of inner stillness I became aware of the aspects to my inner being. The first was my thinking mind. I realised my mind was divided into two parts. One part I called the *mundane mind*. This level of mind dealt with day-to-day affairs and tended to chatter in my head; just like a small child. It usually demanded attention and distracted me with one fascinating thought after another.

As a child needs boundaries, so I realised my mundane mind required training to settle otherwise I was in danger of being dominated by it. The practice of meditation disciplined my mundane mind. I cannot say that it is the choice for everyone or that I have been completely successful in controlling my mind but meditation has been of great benefit to me. When I practice, I find my attachment to insistent thoughts is reduced bringing serenity into my life.

The second part of my mind I called the *inspired mind.* When I relaxed and allowed inner stillness, inspirations came to uplift and inspire me. This was the level of mind that filled me with insights. I was taught to express the inspired mind in satsang, which means 'the company of truth'.

Inspiration could flow into my inspired mind from higher dimensions when I surrendered my attachment to the constant chatter, anxieties, preoccupations, fantasies and addictions of my mundane mind.

I recognised inspiration in Maharaji when he gave satang. Something more profound was expressed through him than the mundanity of normal conversation.

Maharaji recommended the inspired communication of satsang, selfless service and meditation to help me surrender attachment to my mundane thoughts. With my physics I was rarely successful when I tried to think things through. My best insights came when I gave up thinking and allowed space for a solution to pop into my head. I had to make the effort of thinking on a problem to receive inspiration. But the inspiration did not come from the logical sequence of thought. It would pop into a space between thoughts or into the mental silence when the thinking had burnt itself out.

I was well aware of this after waking from sleep with groundbreaking ideas fresh in my mind or re-writing my work to receive expression from the deeper level of my mind. Then there were the insights when I went to the loo. The physical expression of release and flow somehow triggered the a release and flow of ideas in the inspired mind.

I recognised the process as making space in mundane thinking to allow for inspiration to come through. Letting go of thinking allowed for the void of possibilities and through inspired conversations I touched my inner source of wisdom.

I believe many problems in the world stem from the extent to which we allow the mundane mind to dominate our attention. Times of silence and inspired communication create space and opportunity for the inspired mind to express though all of us.

My mundane mind would generate stress through anxieties and imaginings. I learnt from my father to trust all outcomes as perfect. He taught me to relax into the breath. When I trusted I relaxed and that allowed my inspired mind to replace stress with inner peace.

My emotions constituted another aspect of my inner being. I was aware that my feelings empowered my thoughts. My experience was that emotions could be destructive if I allowed my mundane mind to hang onto fear and anger. Letting go and trusting was the antidote to stress; especially around money.

Harnessed to the inspired mind I found my positive emotions could be transformative. I used the analogy of electricity in my satsang. Thoughts I likened to voltage and emotions to current. Combined together they are equivalent to watts, the power in the circuit. I was learning that with the right attitude I had the creative power to manifest inspired thought into reality.

In the mid-1970's, we didn't have as many self-help books and workshops as are available today. They were just emerging. Now the same stream of understanding that came through Maharaji is surfacing in many teachers.

From the late 1960's when the Beatles first embraced meditation, a wave of inspired thought broke on the consciousness of humanity. One of Pa's closest friends, Barry Stonehill, hosted Yogi Maharshi in his Mayfair flat and helped him get established when he first came to London from India. I am still in touch with Barry today and love to hear his tales of his days with Pa and the Beatles' guru.

Yogi Maharshi brought a great wave of yoga from the East. Many waves of yoga were breaking on the shores of the West. In his infancy Maharaji was proclaimed as a born master of yoga. Yoga, the science of union, was bringing me full circle as it was the science of yoga that brought me the vortex.

Union was the aspect of being which I discovered through Knowledge. Knowledge was more than meditation because it enabled me to shift from thinking thoughts, inspired or mundane, to being the awareness of thought. Through Knowledge I came to realise I was not the thoughts I thought I was. I began to identify with the consciousness of my thoughts, my emotions and my bodily sensations. Identifying with my consciousness rather than my thoughts was how I achieved yoga; that is union with my true self.

Descartes said, *"I think therefore I am."*

Obviously Descartes didn't have Knowledge.

Yoga taught me, *"I am therefore I think."*

This new awareness was serendipitous. My exploration of consciousness through Knowledge was vital for my understanding of the Universe.

In science and philosophy I realised there was a lack of clarity. Scientists confused consciousness and mind. Philosophers without Knowledge didn't stop thinking so they never experienced the separation between thought and awareness of thought. When in meditation I stopped thinking, I didn't cease to be so Descartes was definitely wrong when he said existence depends on thinking.

Socrates said, *"Know yourself"*.

I knew that through the Knowledge; that is knowledge of myself, I could comprehend the Universe. True teachers through the ages have taught the gateway to understanding the Universe is to understand ourselves.

I reasoned that if conscious awareness is more fundamental than thought in me then perhaps the same applied to the Universe. Maybe conscious awareness was underlying all energy.

The Copenhagen Interpretation of quantum reality contended that things exist only to the extent they are observed. If this were true, then conscious awareness would underpin the whole of reality.

I realised why thoughts are so demanding of attention. Thought depends on attention to exist. Thoughts only survive when we are aware of them. That is the nature of the abstract. When a thought is banished from consciousness it ceases to be.

I then applied that logic to the Universe. If energy is more thought than thing and everything is formed of energy, then the entire Universe would depend on awareness in order to exist.

I concluded: 'Energy is not the act of a particle: Energy is the act of consciousness'.

I was beginning to see a middle road between religion and science. This line of reasoning excited me. In science the scientist is the prime observer that gives the experiment objective existence. In religion God is the prime observer that gives the Universe objective existence. In the new thinking consciousness is the prime observer and there is no clear demarcation between the mind of man and the mind of God; there is just energy and the awareness of energy.

I then began to wonder whether there was a link between the observer in me and the observer that brings all energy into existence.

I started by thinking about protons. If the proton is an act of consciousness and the consciousness is particulate then each proton would be unique. However, every proton in the Universe is the same as every other proton. That suggested to me that the same consciousness underlies all protons. I reasoned that I am conscious and if consciousness is undivided, then the conscious awareness in me would be the same as in everyone else; it would be the consciousness of the Universe.

It dawned on me that there is only one observer in existence. I had seen a possibility that the observer in me was the same observer in everyone. Looking out of everyone's eyes, hearing through everyone's ears, feeling all feelings, thinking all thoughts this same one consciousness would be imagining the entire Universe into existence.

That was a colossal concept, a totally awesome possibility; worth considering for its sheer potential. It dawned on me we are all one being in many bodies; not in our thinking but in our awareness of thought. Then I understood another great teacher from India.

When questioned if he was God, Sathya Sai Baba replied, "Yes I am God but so are you. The only difference is I know it and you do not."

That was when it all came together for me. We are all one God in many different bodies experiencing unlimited lives with all the joys and pains of human history. Then I understood what it was to be human. In ancient Egyptian the word 'Hu' was the equivalent to our word 'God'. We are the God-man beings.

Thanks to the great Yogic tradition of India I was able to appreciate the words of the Bible: *Be still and know that I am God*. And it was so simple. All I had to do was relax and breathe, surrendering attachment to limiting beliefs and the internal dialogue, and just be my own true self.

Many teachers and teachings influenced me on my exploration into consciousness but fundamental to them all was one profound truth; when we are at peace the consciousness of life is never further than a breath away.

I wrote a song to celebrate all the great spiritual teachers, past and present, from Krishna, Buddha and Christ in ancient times to Sai Baba, Amma and Maharaji in my day and the internal Lord in each and every human heart which is our own true self, our common consciousness and innate divinity:

The love of the Lord makes every moment right,
Makes living worthwhile makes life's burden light,
The love of the Lord brings all things to be,
From each spark of life to the mighty galaxy.
But the love of Our Lord within the human heart,
Means more than the world to Our Lord.

The love of the Lord in the setting of the sun,
In the thunder of the sea, in the busy honey bee,
The love of the Lord in the birds flying south,
In the early morning dew, makes every moment new.
But the love of Our Lord within the human heart,
Means more than the world to Our Lord.

The love of the Lord means more than all the gold,
More than all the power to the priceless human soul,
With the love of the Lord we have more than a king,
More than this world, we have everything
For the love of Our Lord within the human heart,
Means more than the world to Our Lord.

Chapter 20
The Field

"Healing is any non-invasive treatment that stimulates the body to heal itself."

Michael Ash

While he was in London Pa had started to teach the premies how to heal and a number of them wanted to take up a discipline in alternative medicine as a career. In response he decided to found a college of alternative medicine. I wanted to include my work in the college curriculum and so CAMS, the College of Alternative Medicine and Science was born.

Along with weekend Knowledge retreats we ran residential courses for CAMS from Congdons Bridge at Crackington Haven. Pa taught his techniques for healing, manipulations and acupuncture. I taught the vortex physics and Stephen gave lessons in human biology. Several alternative practitioners in the UK can trace the start of their careers to a CAMS course.

Part of my work was to provide a scientific account for healing and alternative medicine. The main book Pa asked me to work from was: *Blueprint for Immortality: The Electric Patterns of Life* by Harold Saxton Burr, an emeritus professor of anatomy at Yale University. Burr devoted twenty years to researching the electrical patterns of life and published over fifty papers in American medical and scientific journals. He discovered minute electrical patterns in and on every living thing he tested, from leaves to newt eggs and human bodies to sprouting seeds. He used very sensitive voltmeters to carry out his measurements because the signals he detected were extremely weak. It was as though he were measuring the shadow of something intangible. Burr called it the electro-dynamic field of life, the life-field or simply the L-field. Burr explained that when we meet a friend after six months to a year not a molecule in their face was there when last we met. Every atom has been replaced from the food we eat. Burr said his extensive research showed that the life field was holding the pattern into which the atoms, molecules and cells fell, to form the familiar face of your friend.

He went onto say that until modern instruments revealed the existence of the controlling L-fields, biologists were at a loss to explain how our bodies 'keep in shape' through ceaseless metabolism and changes of material. Now the mystery had been solved: the electro-dynamic field served as a matrix or mould, which preserved the shape or arrangement of any material poured into it, however often the material was changed.

Pa repeated Burr's work and tested the voltages on plants and animals with the same equipment he devised for ovulation indication. On one occasion, when Pa was measuring the electrical patterns on a pine tree, he picked up a pine needle lying on the ground and chewed on it. The signals went berserk as the pine tree registered distress.

On our CAMS courses we spoke of the *morphic field* - from the Greek word for form. Today this is usually referred to simply as *the field*. We taught that healing and acupuncture treat the body by stimulating the field that holds the form of the body. Pa would say that all he was doing was assisting the body in its own natural ability to heal.

Pa and Dr Felix Mann were the first doctors to practice acupuncture in the UK. In Harley Street Pa used an acupuncture technique he developed himself combining what he had been taught in the 1950's by an acupuncturist from Vietnam and his radiesthesia.

He would move his hands just above the skin of his patient feeling for a tingling sensation and then peer down looking for a small circle of redness on the skin with a pinpoint of white at the center – a pore in the skin. That he would identify as the acupuncture point.

Pa felt the pulse of the patient in the classic way of the acupuncturist to decide if the Chi – the life force energy - required stimulation or sedation. He would stimulate by slipping a gold needle in the open pore at the center of the acupuncture point or sedate with a silver needle.

I remember him demonstrating to the students how the Chi could be stimulated or sedated just by touching the point with the appropriate needle. He called the procedure, 'non-invasive acupuncture' which he classified as healing.

I explained acupuncture to the students using the traditional Chinese analogy of rivers and lakes. But I went further to tell them Chi in the field was *super-energy* - energy beyond light. This overlaid and penetrated the physical body. The *acupuncture meridians* were not channels in the physical body; they were energy flow lines in the field.

Pa taught that the flow of Chi in the meridian was stimulated by gold and sedated by silver. Levels of 'super-energy' Chi in an organ could be increased or decreased through the meridian. The balance of Chi, ascertained by the pulse, influenced the health of the organ connected to the meridian as a lake kept from stagnation by the flow of a river.

Pa also taught the basic principles of homeopathy and showed the students how to potentise their own remedies as he had taught us when we were children. Pa's standard demonstration was to prepare a homeopathic medicine for hay fever. It was fun on the CAMS courses repeating the lessons of our childhood. We crushed grass in a mortar and pestle to make a mother liquor that would set any sufferer sneezing. We then diluted that one in ten in water and shook the solution one hundred times. Pa called that 1x. We then diluted one part of 1x in ten parts of water and shook it again a hundred times to make a 2x potentisation. We diluted and shook 2x in the same way to make 3x and continued the procedure until we had a 6x potency. That was the first level of dilution that reversed the symptoms of hay fever. As the remedy was further diluted and potentised it became increasingly effective in relieving hay fever.

I explained the homeopathic process to the students by way of photography as an analogy. The super-energy field of the grass liquor that caused the hay fever was the equivalent of a positive image. Shaking this in the water produced a negative of the image in the super-energy field of the water. Diluting and potentising the remedy then increased the negative pattern in the water that negated the symptoms of hay fever.

I stressed that acupuncture and homeopathy were super-energy medicine. They had everything to do with physics and very little to do with chemistry. Materialistic scientists couldn't make sense of these alternative treatments because they attempted to explain everything in terms of material particles rather than energy fields.

I did a lot of teaching on the spectacular cliffs of Crackington looking out over the grand sweep of the North Atlantic. Pointing to the horizon I told the students that just as Columbus had to contend with flat-earth mentality of medieval Europe where people believed the horizon was the end of the world so alternative medicine though effective, was dismissed by most doctors because they were stuck with the outmoded materialistic worldview of science.

As we watched the stately progress of the waves rolling in from the south, I compared them with waves of Chi, the super-energy in the field enfolding the cell.

I explained that just as radio waves resonate with the coil in a radio set so does Chi resonate with the DNA molecule in the cell. DNA in the nucleus of the cell is a coil and it is that DNA coil that resonates with the field.

A few years later I developed the concept of DNA resonance more fully. The idea was that information was broadcast from higher dimensions as frequencies in the field surrounding a cell. The DNA double helix is wound in coils to form chromosomes which resonate with these frequencies. That, I suggested, was the key to creative evolution.

I reckoned the DNA molecule could be modified by information coming into the field. I speculated that what biologists took to be random mutations were in fact design additions to DNA operated through super-energy resonance.

I explained that DNA was very stable and unlikely to change. Genetic modifications came by adding more codes to the double helix strands rather than changing what was already there. Each new addition to the codes was an improvement on the old. I contended that was why we all have 'dinosaur DNA' in our cells. I argued most of our DNA is unused because the information on it is extinct. It wasn't, however, completely useless because it built up the coil structure for DNA resonance.

My main concern at CAMS was not evolution but differentiation. Differentiation is the mysterious process that sorts cells into different organs and tissues. All cells in the body originate from a single cell at conception. The conundrum confronting biologists was to explain how it was that one cell became skin and another muscle or bone? I was using my physics to provide an account for differentiation through DNA resonance.

Professor Burr proved that it was more where a cell was in the electro-dynamic field of life than what it was genetically that determined what it would become. He did this in a series of simple and yet ingenious experiments. He worked with undifferentiated cells in newt eggs - the bundle of cells that form immediately after fertilization.

In an egg it is possible to predict which end of the early embryo will grow into a head and which will grow into a tail. To begin with Burr sliced cells off the presumptive head end and grafted them onto the tail end and sat back to watch. Would he hatch a monster newt with a head growing out of its bottom? No, an amphibian monster wasn't born. A perfectly normal newt hatched out of its egg and swam away.

In the next experiment Professor Burr placed a newt egg in a powerful electric field that forced the electro-dynamic field within the egg to reverse direction. He watched the embryo grow under the microscope. The cells that should have developed into a head grew into a tail and those that should have grown into a tail grew into a head. Again no monster newt was born. However, the normal newt grew in its egg the wrong way round.

The DNA in every cell of the body is the same. In his experiments Burr proved it is not *what* a cell is genetically but *where* it is in the field that determines what it will become.

There is no doubt that the chemistry of DNA is important in storing hereditary information in the genes but what I realised all those years ago was the importance of the physics of DNA forming the chromosome as a coil. The chromosome coil resonating with the field had a vital part to play; if not the most important part to play in genetics.

My belief was that the field is a pattern of frequencies corresponding to the shape of the physical body and that cells take up the shape as they resonate to the frequencies specific to their place in the field. Through DNA resonance each frequency would influence a different gene causing the cell to differentiate or perform as required. This all depended on wherever it happened to be in the field of frequencies.

Treating the frequency patterns as thought forms allowed for a greater influence of the mind and emotions on our genetic make up than materialistic biology permitted. If thoughts and emotions could influence the field then by DNA resonance our thoughts, beliefs and attitudes could have a profound effect on our physical bodies.

On the CAMS courses we taught that the morphic field was not restricted to biological organisms. We gave the pattern of a snowflake as an example of a non-organic field at work. Emphasizing water is a liquid crystal I speculated that as a crystal it could resonate with super-energy fields; much as crystals in the cat-whisker radio sets we build with Pa when we were children resonated with radio broadcasts. I suggested it was the crystalline patterns in the water - and sugar crystals - that held the impression of the substances used to make homeopathic remedies. From homeopathy it was clear that water had the capacity to hold thought patterns as frequencies in the field.

I began to wonder whether other forms of matter might store psychic energy in the same way. I began to realise how the psychosphere worked. If the super-energy fields overshadowing things could store thought patterns, through resonance with our own fields we could pick these up. We taught the need to be conscious of the things we were hording because the psychic energies they were storing could have a detrimental effect on us.

At CAMS we used the 'physics of the field' to explain why for a healthy body we needed a positive frame of mind, balanced emotions and attitude of detachment. This approach made a lot of sense to the premies who understood the danger of negative thoughts and emotions and the importance of non-attachment to material things in order to find inner peace.

From our understanding of resonance and the field, we also reasoned that the collective human field could only switch from war to peace through the impact of millions of individual fields vibrating in harmony with love and forgiveness. That is why the teaching of the great spiritual masters was so profound. Only by the majority of people finding peace within would there be lasting peace in the world outside.

The DNA Double Helix forming a Chromosome Coil

Chapter 21
Popping in on the Pope

"A heart full of gold is worth more than all the gold in the world."

Michael Ash

In November 1977, Maharaji was holding a festival in Rome. Anna and I were planning to go along with Ma and Pa and everything was going smoothly until Pa exclaimed, "It's a pity to go all the way to Rome without visiting the Pope."

Ma shrieked; "We were going to see Maharaji not the Pope!"

Pa told me that high frequency deafness common in men was feature of evolution. He explained that chaps who were deaf to the high pitch voices of their wives survived marriage better than those with perfect hearing and that gave them a breeding advantage. This trait, essential to male survival, they passed onto their offspring, and as a result of natural selection, most men on the planet are now deaf to the shrill shrieks of their women folk.

Thus it was Pa never heard Ma's screams of protest and on his instruction I went ahead and wrote to Archbishop Heim who sent back a letter for us to show at the Vatican. He said it would be sufficient to secure us a private audience with Pope Paul VI.

When we arrived in Rome, Pa rang the Vatican. They insisted it was impossible to secure an audience at such short notice. Pa was as deaf to officials as he was to Ma and he didn't speak Italian so he assured them his letter was sufficient and we were coming to meet the Pope the following morning!

So it was the following morning Pa and Ma, me, Anna, baby Becky plus an interpreter piled into a tiny Fiat and hammered across Rome to the Vatican. On arrival Pa waved the letter from the Apostolic Delegate under the nose of a Swiss guard who escorted us to somewhere behind the Basilica of St Peter. My ego was busting through my jacket as we strode with the Swiss Guard past all the tourists. We were greeted into the bowels of the Vatican by a butler in tails who responded favourably to the letter. He led us up in an ante room where we were faced with a pair of enormous, tall doors. Ma and Anna put on headscarves and I adjusted the Tibetan yak-hair jacket I habitually wore for such occasions.

Suddenly the doors swung open to reveal a distant figure in white with red booties, seated on an ornate chair at the end of a vast hall. He was surrounded by men in black with red or purple sashes.

We were completely unprepared. None of us had a clue what to do. Anna was in front of me so I put my hand to the small of her back and gave her a shove. She sailed down the hall, straight up to the Pope took his outstretched hand and shook it.

There were gasps of horror from the surrounding prelates. She was supposed to kneel and kiss the papal ring! Running along behind her I desperately wanted to fall on my knees, beg for absolution on her behalf and kiss the ring but that was impossible because I was holding Becky. The baby had to be given to someone to free up my hands so I handed her to the nearest lap. It was something I did habitually at home and in the panic I went into automatic.

That is how Pope Paul VI ended up with Becky on his lap. My attempt at etiquette was frustrated as the Pope's hands were no longer free to offer me his ring. The faces in the group surrounding the throne were the colour of their sashes but His Holiness was delighted.

Watching the Pontiff laugh at the chuckling baby on his knee, was one of those brief, unscheduled moments of magic one never forgets. It was over almost as quickly as it had begun. Pope Paul gave her a kiss then handed Becky back to her mother and offered me his ring.

Ma was next and finally Pa. We were told afterwards we did it all wrong. It should have been Pa first, and then Ma, followed by me then Anna but the Pope didn't seem to mind. He was beaming the whole time.

The Vicar of Christ then called Ma and Anna back. As they knelt before him he grasped their hands and spoke in fluent English about the importance of motherhood. He blessed Ma for the family she had reared and then turning to Anna he said, "I can see you are a good mother. You are doing the most important work in the world, loving and caring for your children. Never underestimate your role as a mother. Mothers are entrusted was the next generation of humanity. It is a great trust and a grave responsibility."

After the audience we had just settled at a café in the Plaza outside the Basilica of St Peter to enjoy a cup of coffee when Pa recognised a scruffy fellow rummaging through a litter bin. He was the chap Pa had befriended when we visited a place of Marian apparitions called San Damiano near Milan, a couple of years earlier.

The man was well known for harassing the clergy because the apparitions were not recognized by the Church. Pa was certain they were authentic because he had a vision of Mary in which she expressed her concern for young people.

He said her words to him were: "Unless you catch the blossom there will be no fruit."

My father had said to me, "David I follow Maharaji because he is leading your generation away from drugs and alcohol to Knowledge and is teaching you all to speak words of wisdom instead of meaningless chatter."

Pa also believed in Maharaji because at San Damiano Mary had said, "A great light will come from the East and it will come from outside the Church."

As he looked at the champion of San Damiano hunt through the trash for food, Pa was fingering the papal medal he had just been given by the Pope. Turning to me with a smile on his face he said, "I think I can see someone who deserves this medal more than me!"

Before I could say anything to restrain him Pa jumped up from his seat and strode across to the tramp. He lifted the solid gold from his neck and hung it round the neck of the vagrant. The man gazed in amazement down at the medal and then up at his unexpected benefactor. Taking him firmly by the shoulders Pa said he was passing the medal from the Pope onto him because of his work for Mary at San Damiano.

The gesture was extraordinary as it was insane. Pa was laughing as he returned to his seat, "A heart full of gold is worth more than all the gold in the world. With that medal he will be off to harangue the nearest bishop!"

Ma ever the cynic commented, "It's more likely he'll be off with it to the nearest pawn shop!"

Whatever the man did with that medal was irrelevant. It was Pa's spontaneous generosity of spirit that mattered. With his heart of gold he had no need for medals of gold.

Anna didn't fail the Pope. After our twins Josephine and Jessica, born in November 1975, Becky had come in January 1977 and then in February 1979 Sam arrived.

The Ash family with Pope Paul VI

Anna

The House that David Built

Mary as she appeared miraculously on Polaroid at San Damiano in Italy

In the spring of 1977 we had moved into a tumbledown shack we bought on a piece of land near Week St Mary in North Cornwall. I had put aside my typewriter and picked up a trowel to transform the hovel into a habitable cottage. I tore down the sheets of galvanized iron and plastic and replaced them with walls of stone, I had collected by hand, and pretty cottage windows. I never bothered the planners or building inspectors so they never bothered me. I just got on and built the walls up to two foot thick in places. The eves ended up an inch above the door lintel which made the cottage front low and old worldly in appearance. Building regulations homogenize the landscape and make every dwelling boringly normal. Mine was charmingly different.

We had a tap but no mains electric. The generator was too noisy so we used candles and paraffin lamps. We did everything by hand. I built without power tools and Anna cooked on the old wood burning Rayburn. I built the bath up on blocks so Anna didn't have to bend over when bathing the babies. That was filled with water from kettles on the stove. As for the loo, that was Centrepoint!

An enormous plastic composting toilet arrived one day on the back of a lorry. I hadn't ordered it. The company had no record of sending it and as there was no invoice, no payment was required.

The challenge was setting it up. Our land was waterlogged clay on the flat so the bog couldn't be dug into the ground. Instead the huge plastic chamber was planted by the hedge, surrounded by a hurriedly built block wall and crowned with a tatty tin shed.

Our environmentally friendly loo didn't impress our friends. The sheets of recycled rusty old iron and cracked mould covered Perspex rattled in the wind. Going to the toilet in winter was a dash of desperation. In summer, a cloud of flies would rise to greet us. The children stuck to their potties.

My younger brother Peter and his Cornish-gypsy wife Muriel had settled in a cottage a few miles down the road. They had no electric and only a well for water but their ancient dwelling, hidden amongst the trees, was so full of magic Muriel could see the fairies

Anna and I produced a fairy tale book based on my vortex physics called *The Tower of Truth*. Anna drew the illustrations and CAMS published it. We launched the book at the first Festival of Mind Body and Spirit in Olympia but the remnant stock found its way onto the bed of Sumo, Peter and Muriel's Vietnamese pig. Peter was storing them for me then moved the pig into the store. Eating my books, Sumo must have been the first pig in history to digest the theory of relativity.

Chapter 22
Steven's Story

The most important law in medicine is absent from every medical textbook, that the difference between dead tissue and living tissue is that living tissue heals itself.

Michael Ash

In the 1960's, Pa's book *Health Radiation and Healing* had been published by Darton, Longman and Todd and in 1976 Pa received a letter from a Dale Goldstein at the Zen Centre in Rochester NY. He had been sent a copy of Pa's book by a Richard Roberts from Down-to-Earth, Greenwich City N. Y. Dale offered to set up a coast to coast healing workshop tour for Pa, but immediately Pa offered the opportunity to me. As I had no ambition to abandon my new wife and twin babies I suggested he offer the tour to Steven.

Steven, disillusioned with teaching in the London schools, jumped at the opportunity and left for New York as soon as his bags were packed and ticket procured. He launched with enthusiasm on a whirlwind tour of New York, Rochester, Boston and Washington before heading off to Texas where he taught Pa's healing techniques and energy medicine in Dallas, Houston and Fort Worth. Then he drove to California where his bubble of sanctity burst. On a silent, spiritual retreat, the cook out on an early morning jog discovered naughty Steven on the top of a mountain in a sleeping bag with a girl. He fled in disgrace to Eugene Oregon where overcome with stress and exhaustion he had a fit in a cinema. Dale contacted Pa. Pa said he would come out immediately and Dale sent him a one way ticket to San Francisco.

When Pa arrived at the airport he was asked how much money he had. He said he had none. Where was he going? He replied to visit his son in Eugene. Did he have an address? No! It is still a mystery how he was let into the USA.

Those were the days before emails and mobile phones and Pa had no idea where Steven was in Eugene. He arrived in the city late in the evening and went up to a biker saying he was looking for his son who had a motor bike back in the UK. The biker took Pa pillion and spent the rest of the night helping him search for Steven. They located him through posters in the city thus Steven was woken in the early hours by the unexpected Pa trailing a Hells Angel.

Pa worked with Steven on the remainder of his West Coast tour running healing workshops in Oregon then at the Eselan Institute in Big Sur after which they continued to Santa Cruz and Los Angeles in California.

Somewhere in Oregon, Steven and Pa were invited to a council of Native American Chiefs who assembled in a circle of chairs. After a while Pa got off his chair and sat on the floor. All the chiefs got off their chairs and sat on the floor. Pa then slid down and lay on his side. All the chiefs slid down and lay on their sides. Pa then rolled onto his back and fell asleep. All the chiefs then broke into laughter. Someone explained to Steven afterwards that it was a tradition amongst them that the greatest chief sat at the lowest level so rather than accept Pa as the greatest chief they all had to get down to his level.

As Steven and Pa drove into California they were shocked by the arid condition of the State which had been stricken with drought. Despite the cloudless sky Pa decided to make it rain. Steven was driving with a woman called Yanna while Pa lay in the back of her VW micro bus visualising rain. Within an hour black, threatening clouds began to appear in the sky and soon heavy drops were hitting the windscreen. Minutes later it was raining so hard the drops was bouncing off the road. Pa just lay in the back laughing.

At Santa Cruz, Pa conducted a healing for mothers and asked everyone in the room to meditate on their mother. Steven tuned into Ma and picked up she was distressed. When he told Pa, Pa decided go home immediately and was about to leave when two women in the group, who were Rosicrucians and fruitarians, offered to take him back to their place so he could phone her instead. Ma told him the bank was foreclosing because no money had been paid in for months. When Pa relayed the cause of Ma's distress the women got out a cheque book and asked him how much he needed to clear the bank loan. He replied £18,000. They wrote out a check for the equivalent in dollars and in a stroke of the pen the outstanding debt on the house, which had burdened parents for years, was cleared.

The next destination was the Berkley Holistic Health Centre. There Steven met a Canadian girl called Shane. Pa decided to leave them to it and return to the UK.

Steven and Shane headed off to Bolder Colorado for the 1977 Rocky Mountain Healing Festival where they bought a ford falcon van and drove back to New York for another East Coast teaching tour organised by Dale. Unfortunately Dale and Shane clashed and as the weather was turning cold Steven decided to break free of Dale and set up his own tour with Shane in the sunny south so heading off for Florida they didn't stop until they got to Key West. By the time they arrived Steven was wishing he were back on his own working with Dale but Shane didn't want to leave him so they decided to pray a Novena of Rosaries (nine days of prayer) for their relationship.

Meanwhile, unbeknown to Steven, Pa, Ma and Richard had arrived in New York where Pa picked up with Dale and Richard Roberts and Professor John Mosher of Rochester. But Ma quickly bored of New York in the freezing cold and said she would like to join Steven. She asked Dale where he was but Dale didn't know apart from Steven saying they were heading for the sun. The sun appealed to Ma and so she asked Pa to help. Pa didn't have a clue, nonetheless he lay down to meditate. After a few minutes he sat up and told Ma to head south as far as she could go and then enter the first Catholic church she saw. There she would find Steven.

Ma and Richard set off forthwith in a Greyhound bus and eventually landed in Key West; the southernmost place in the United States of America. When they arrived they settled for the night in a motel. The following morning Ma got up and went for a walk and lo and behold she spotted a Catholic church. She entered just in time for the early morning Mass.

Steven and Shane had decided to attend Mass every morning during their Novena and were seated in the front pews of that very church. Shane happened to glance round and spotted Ma at the back. She hissed to Steven, "Hey, your mom's in the back row."

"Don't be stupid, Ma is in Cornwall." whispered Steven continuing his beads.

Shane looked round again, "Steven I'm sure that's your mother at the back. I recognise her from the photograph."

"Shut-up Shane, I told you Ma is in Cornwall now let me pray, will you!" Steven retorted in an irritated whisper.

A few minutes passed and Shane glanced round again. This time the mystery lady smiled and waved. Shane elbowed Steven, "Look round yourself and see, it's definitely your mom, she waved at me!"

Steven turned round. Shock then exhilaration crossed his face in quick succession. It was Ma. That was the magic of his parents and the manifest power of prayer because the answer to the Novena followed very quickly.

The following night, Steven and Shane were awoken in the night by police hammering on the door of their van. They were arrested for sleeping in the open and taken into custody for the weekend until court convened on Monday morning where Steven explained to the judge, "In England, Sir, we have an expression; *an Englishman's home is his castle.* That van is my home so I was sleeping in my castle not in the open."

The judge, amused by the English eccentricity let them go free but when they got back to Ma, she was furious with Steven for running off with his popsy for the weekend when she and Richard had just arrived from New York. Not for a minute did she believe his cock and bull story of their being locked up in separate cells for the weekend and told him to marry the girl and stop messing around. Knowing better than to argue with Ma when she was so angry, Steven proposed to Shane and she accepted.

They were married in that self same church. Pa came down from New York and Shane's family from Ottawa. Pa then returned with Ma and Richard to New York leaving Steven to his marital fate and wondering why on earth he had decided to pray!

Shane then decided she wanted to visit Cornwall so the van was sold and they headed for New York. In JFK airport Steven was hobbling in pain due to a knee injury.

Suddenly up strolled Pa. He sat Steven down, healed his knee with his miraculous healing power and collecting his bus fare back into the city from Steven's purse, disappeared as mysteriously as he had appeared.

Pa kept doing that to Steven. That was their medicine together. It never happened to me that way. Pa didn't work magic like that with me. For me Pa worked the mystery in radioactivity physics and that turned out to be awesome.

Chapter 23
My Family Life

Every life when truly lived is a story of faith

Michael Ash

Anna and I decided our cottage in North Cornwall was too isolated so as soon as the renovations were finished we sold up and moved to Millbrook to join a community of premies in East Cornwall. Nestled in the green hills of the Rame peninsula, Millbrook is a picturesque village separated from the city of Plymouth by the Tamar estuary. There I entered the world of direct sales.

Selling is an empowering experience where mistakes lead to personal growth. The learning curve for me was substantial in the hard interface between people and corporations, and I thrived on it. For someone with a head residing in the esoteric clouds of physics and metaphysics marketing life insurance from door to door was grounding.

I also opened a nutrition practice and had spectacular results in healing through adjusting people's diets from processed food to whole foods. A favourable feature in the *Western Morning News* led to my appearing with my ideas as a nutritionist on the *Nationwide* TV magazine programme following the early evening BBC news.

We stayed in Millbrook for eighteen months. It was there I wrote my signature tune:

Love is the answer, love is the hope,
Love is the only thing that can save us in this world,
Love is the key to open up the heart,
Love is the place where life really starts.
But love isn't given with a wedding ring
Love isn't given when a singer sings,
Love alone from the soul will spring,
Unexpected, unreasoned,
Usually a fleeting passing thing,
But love endless love,
In a flood that knows no bounds,
Will gush forth from the soul,
And will sweep the world around,
If the soul is only open,
Like a flower in the spring,
And the mind if it's harnessed,
That wild heartless thing,
And devotion if given with love from the heart,
In an instant we'll be given love eternal love,
Love eternal love, Love eternal love.

Living on my wits at the edge of broke, I couldn't afford the luxury of being impractical. I had to build and decorate, and mend motor cars. Physical labour kept me balanced. I thrived as a down to earth handyman. It helped me to support my large growing family.

Then I decided the grass is greener on the other side of the Atlantic. Like father like son, I decided to leave England for America. Anna conceded to the adventure so we disposed of all our possessions, sold the home to clear the backlog of debt and flew off to Canada to visit Stephen and Shane in Ottawa were they were living in with their little boy Devon, a few months younger than Sam.

As Maharaji was scheduled to do a programme in Kansas City followed by birthday celebrations in Miami we planned a trip from Ontario to Florida via Kansas. Anna had friends in Trinidad and Tobago so we booked to fly on to the Caribbean on Christmas Eve.

After a month with Stephen and Shane we set off in a Dodge Auto Home with three toddler daughters, their dolls and a bouncing little boy clinging to 'monkey' with its one glass and one button eye. Progress across the States was slow because of the innumerable breakdowns of the dodgy Dodge and stops at practically every play-park on route. But we arrived at Kansas City in time for Maharaji's programme and eventually we made it to Miami in time for his birthday party on December 10th 1980.

A friend called Marek had flow in from Brighton for the celebrations. An acupuncturist who originally attended our CAMS courses, he gave me his card and invited me to join his practice as a nutritionist. Anna welcomed the idea of settling on the south coast of Sussex on our return to the UK so we could live close to her parents.

On Christmas Eve we arrived at Miami airport to catch our flights to Trinidad, only to discover the travel agent in Canada had not forwarded our tickets as arranged. The women at checkout were implacable. Though our names were on the flight list, we had no tickets so there was no way they would let us catch that flight.

We were a forlorn family facing Christmas in an airport terminal when suddenly the normally placid and tolerant Anna shape-shifted into a raging lioness. I had never seen anything like it before; neither had girls behind the checking counter. They were terrified and boarding passes were hurriedly issued. Kids and dolls bundled under arm, the blonde whirlwind swept all before her and we ran in her wake onto the aircraft minutes before the gate closed.

With our four children we enjoyed the delight of a tropical Christmas with a family in Trinidad where generosity and open heartedness are a national characteristic. They insisted we stay for carnival so we stopped on for ten weeks which gave me ample opportunity to write.

The major challenge for me was to secure a mango for myself from the tree overhanging the veranda where I worked. I watched the mangoes closely as they ripened. The trick was stealth. The net on a long pole for hooking mangoes had to be manipulated without so much as rustling a leaf but it never worked. Every time I landed a juicy fruit in the net four little faces would appear round the corner. No matter how busy they were at play or how far they were away never once did the movement of the net in the mango tree ever go unnoticed. After the carnival, where exotic troupes in erotic costumes surged on mass through the streets of Port of Spain, swinging to the sound of evocative steel bands, we returned to England.

We landed in March 1981 with no possessions and just enough money to put down as a rental bond on a house. After settling my exhausted family into a hotel in Brighton I went searching for accommodation. By the time they awoke I had secured a furnished home opposite the church built by William the Conqueror at Shoreham by sea.

Anna and the children headed for her parents leaving me to drop leaflets in Hove and Brighton, advertising a migraine clinic. Walking garden paths and smelling the roses helped me reconnect with England.

My nutrition treatments for migraine through diet were so successful I started weekend courses for dieticians to pass on my techniques. These were well attended and supplemented the practice income. Anna's job was to empty the purse. My job was to fill it.

We had a wonderful summer in Shoreham and celebrated our return to England with the conception of another baby. Anna wasn't as jubilant as me as she thought her family was complete with four children!

With the autumn we relocated to a family house along the coast in Worthing with sea views from our bedroom window and a large garden complete with Wendy house and swings for the children. There, on our seventh wedding anniversary, Ondine was born.

Stephen's marriage to Shane had broken down so he returned to England and moved in with us. It was wonderful having him back in our lives. A big overgrown puppy, he kept the children continually amused. We practiced meditation, ran satsang meetings and made music together. Anna added keyboards and her voice to a set of recordings for which I wrote a new song:

With every beat of the human heart,
There's the purest drop of love,
To bind every human heart into a garland,
Of love to stretch the world around,
Oh a garland of love to stretch the world around.

With every ebb and flood of tide,
There's a hope for the world,
To survive the darkest time in all the ages,
If only we can find our drop of love,
Oh if only everyone can find their drop of love.

With every breath that comes and goes,
There's a treasure beyond,

All things we can see and touch with this human frame,
If only we can search our heart within,
Oh if only everyone can search their heart within.

With every beat of the human heart,
There's the purest drop of love,
To bind every human heart into a garland,
Of love to stretch the world around,
Oh a garland of love to stretch the world around.

An elderly gentleman called Jack who attended our meetings and came to our garden parties lent me a deposit and helped me arrange a mortgage so that Anna and I could buy our own home. I chose a house for the walnut tree in the garden and couldn't be bothered to look inside as I was only interested in the tree. The agents were flabbergasted. They had never sold a house before without a viewing but Anna insisted on looking the inside before signing. Nowt stranger than women; fancy not being satisfied by the walnut tree in the garden with all its potential for swings and tree houses!

Worthing was good for me. The south coast of Sussex nurtured my soul. Strolling along the sticky, seaweed-strewn beach one day I began to think again about the theory of evolution. It must have been the smell of seaweed that got me mulling over the primordial slime.

I began to muse about the early days of the Earth when there were no people, animals or plants; only atoms. If particles of energy were more thoughts than things then it struck me light could carry information and atoms store it.

I imagined one informed atom bumping into another and reacting to form a molecule. That would be two atomic ideas combining to form a molecular memory. I loved to think of molecules as memories. It had struck me long before that light was the equivalent of thought, transmitting information and matter memory, storing information.

The stench of rotting seaweed focused my attention on intelligent evolution and I began to think of DNA as a self-replicating molecular memory. DNA was the combination of molecules in a mirror symmetrical double helix 'vortex' strand that allowed a molecular memory code to be replicated. For me the replication of molecular memory was all important as it was the key to life on Earth.

As I walked on the beach of Worthing it was clear to me that through the evolution of DNA the Universal mind had shifted to another level. The DNA vortex allowed the memories we perceive as life on earth to evolve and grow, replicate and develop in remarkable ways.

But then, after the 1983 general election I diverted my attention from evolution to electoral reform. I was appalled at the lack of representation in Britain. The spread of votes between parties in the 1983 election was not represented in the distribution of seats between parties in parliament so I decided to do something about it. I devised a new electoral system based on a hybrid of proportional representation and the traditional first past the post system. I called it HER – Hybrid Electoral Reform. Applied to the results of the 1983 election to my system would have given the new Liberal Democrat alliance fair representation in the House of Commons while still allowing the Conservatives an overall majority with which to govern.

I sent copies of my paper on electoral reform to MPs, the Electoral Reform Society and other people who were influential in politics. It took off like a rocket in a barrel of water. I got a few polite replies of acknowledgment and a baroness from the House of Lords replied that she didn't like hybrids.

The only person who took me seriously was an eccentric retired barrister in Worthing. He was a life long liberal and published the results of my system his own journal for the Liberal Party Conference. Nothing came of the effort but I did my bit for Democracy.

Anna was very patient. Most wives would have nagged their husbands to go out and get a job instead of spending months on non-productive projects but Anna never harassed me. She fed me, loved me and let me alone to get on with whatever I was doing because she knew it was important to me. Thus I was able to follow the breakthrough into nuclear energy and the strong nuclear force when it came.

When proton vortices converge in the sun or a hydrogen bomb, energy swirling inside them is displaced. That is nuclear energy.

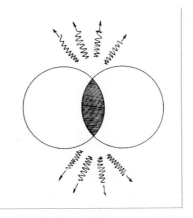

The remaining energy left behind swirls between the converged vortices binding them together. That is the strong nuclear force

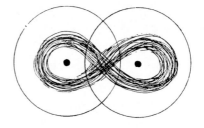

Chapter 24
The Figure of Eight

"To accomplish all keep on going even when all hope appears lost."

Michael Ash

Steve Walker ran a house clearance and antique business close to where we lived in East Worthing. After attending one or two of our satsang meetings he became a good friend. I whiled away many an hour discussing philosophy and metaphysics at his shop and it was Steve who encouraged me to set up the holistic health association that led to the resurrection of my physics. It all began when Pa and I were invited to represent the holistic health association at a conference at Cirencester chaired by Sir George Trevelyan. Pa knew Sir George and introduced me to the grand old man who, remembering me for the copy of *The Tower of Truth* he had received at Olympia, took me under his wing.

He said I had an important task in the world but I needed to learn to speak in public because my delivery at the conference was deplorable. If I could organise a talk at Worthing he would come and share the platform with me then he could tutor me in public speaking. So it was I booked The Assembly Rooms in Worthing and advertised a Saturday afternoon program. The event was well attended and under the watchful eye of Sir George Trevelyan, I delivered my lecture.

Anna and the children attended the event to serve teas and Anna met a couple called Brian and Anne Hayman. She visited them after the lecture and spoke enthusiastically about my physics. They were fascinated and arranged to meet me to find out more because she wanted to introduce me to the Marquis of Northampton. Within a week I was invited to London to relay my vortex theory to Lord Northampton in person. When he opened the door I was greeted with "My God it's John Cleese!"

After listening to my presentation he took me out to lunch where I enjoyed my first taste of truffles. He said what I was doing was important and admired me for sticking with it for so many years. He offered to do what he could to help but he would need a professional physicist to give an opinion before he could proceed. He said he would cover the cost of having the work printed in a format that would be presentable and asked me to find someone who would be favourably disposed to examine the work.

After lunch we returned to his flat and over a cup of tea, he looked across to me and asked, "Where is the figure of eight in your physics?"

I was taken aback by the question and began to search my mind for figures of eight. I suggested it must be the infinity sign representing the infinite cycle of vortex energy between matter and anti-matter.

"No, no," exclaimed Lord Northampton, "It's not that!" Then he laughed, "You will find it, don't worry!"

The following evening I was in my favourite chair in a corner of the dining room lost in thought. My mind was preoccupied with the mystery of the figure of eight. The children were eating at the table and a plate of food was passed to me. Absent mindedly I squirted the ketchup over the peas in the form of a figure of eight! Then I saw it. The peas on my plate were protons jostling in the nucleus and the ketchup was energy flowing between them, binding them together.

Lord Northampton had handed me a key to open a door in my mind. Ketchup on the peas flung it open to reveal the vista of nuclear physics. It would take me years to make sense of it all but the process had begun.

It was so obvious I found it hard to believe that I hadn't seen it before. From the *as it is above so it is below* principle protons and neutrons were mini black holes that captured energy in their spiral space paths in the microcosm as did massive black holes in the macrocosm.

I ran upstairs and began to draw. A proton vortex emerged under my pen. Between the lines the spiral space path was apparent. A wave train of energy raced across the paper, down the spiral road, and disappeared into the heart of the vortex particle.

With the life span of a proton estimated at a billion, trillion, trillion years there was ample opportunity for it to capture energy. In that enormous length of time every proton and neutron vortex in existence would have captured as much energy as it could possibly hold. The space in every proton and neutron would be saturated with energy.

The children were playing before bedtime and Anna was preparing their bath. I drew a picture of the captured energy swirling inside the proton. It was immediately obvious the captured spin was contributing to the mass of the nuclear particle. I penned a second proton vortex flying toward the first as it would in the sun or a hydrogen bomb. An immense force is required to cause protons to converge but in the sun or a hydrogen bomb they are moving so fast they collide with sufficient impact to drive into each another.

I then drew another picture with the two vortices overlapping to represent protons converging in nuclear fusion. As the protons collided each vortex converged into the space of the other. On converging, the combined inner space of the proton vortices was reduced. Some of the captured energy was squeezed out.

Anna was busy with Sam getting him into the bath but he kept leaping out of the tub and running away. Suddenly he burst into my room. I picked him up, wet and slippery and dropped him back in the bath with his squealing sisters but as soon as I turned my back he was up and away and the chase began all over again.

When Sam was captured in the bathtub he was fine. But as soon as he got out, he was off as fast as his little legs could carry him. Captured energy in the nuclear particle was just like Sam. As soon as it escaped capture from the converging protons it was off, radiating away as gamma rays, light and heat.

That was the energy released in a nuclear bomb.

In our nuclear family, Sam was running round shrieking. Josephine and Jessica, trying to do their homework were screaming after him, Anna was shouting to calm them down while putting on Ondine's nappy and Ondine was howling because she never liked having her nappy changed. I had just explained nuclear energy. I didn't need to run naked like Archimedes, yelling 'eureka', Sam was doing that for me!

I grabbed the little rascal in a fluffy white bath towel and bundled him in my arms. Throwing him on the sofa I blew bubbles on his chubby tummy until he squealed for me to stop. Laughing, I carried him up to the bedroom. I was so excited I could hardly contain myself. I had to join in the jamboree of bedtime to requite my energy.

Becky, picking up on the excitement, was in my arms for a cuddle. I tickled her until she was squealing with laughter. Sam was shouting for his turn while Ondine toddled into the fray.

Bringing her ubiquitous aura of calm, Anna appeared and established order. Ondine was extracted. Rolling on her siblings she dispelled any inclination they had to settle. Quiet was established, thumbs popped into mouths and big eyes implored a story.

Reading from the magic story book helped us all to calm down! The magic enabled a new story to appear every time we opened the tatty tome so long as we didn't read more than one a night. That would break the spell! By the time I had finished, Sam and Becky were asleep, Sam with one-eyed monkey in his arms and Becky cuddling the shorn Alice; her favourite doll that had recently suffered a drastic hair do. Josephine and Jessica were starting their bed routine and Anna had placed a cup of tea and digestive biscuit on my desk. I was settling Ondine to sleep but I couldn't wait to get back to draw the next picture. It depicted two converged protons with the evicted nuclear energy radiating away.

As I drew, I thought of the children in the bath tub swirling together in the water. One managed to escape but two were left behind. That is how I imagined it in the protons after they collided. As they converged they lost some of their captured energy but most of it was left swirling inside them. That remaining energy, no longer spinning around the centre of a single proton, would be surging inside the two converged protons. I imagined the shape of the captured energy swirling around the two proton centres as something like a peanut. In cross section it was a figure of eight!

The light racing round the centres of the two particles of matter would bind them together. I had drawn a picture of the strong nuclear force. I had waited a decade to uncover nuclear binding and it had just appeared under my pen.

I deduced that if the protons converged even closer, as occurred after nuclear fission in the atomic bomb, more nuclear energy would be squeezed out but because the distance between the nuclear particles was reduced the remaining captured energy would run in a shorter race track and so bind them together more tightly. That explained one of the greatest mysteries in physics; why nuclear binding increased as nuclear mass was lost.

The next day my drawings were on their way to Lord Northampton with a letter describing the discovery. He replied immediately encouraging me to complete the paper for review as quickly as possible.

I located a retired professor of physics through the Medical and Scientific Network who I thought would be supportive, but predictably he dismissed my work and Lord Northampton wrote to say there was nothing more he could do to help me. His plan to introduce my work to Prince Charles was abandoned.

I never met the Marquis of Northampton again but one comment he made stayed with me, "Raise the question but don't give the answer; people have to discover that for themselves."

He did send me the critique. The physics expert said nothing positive about my work. There was only objection and the main criticism was my account for the neutron. I was discredited for treating it as a bound state of electron and proton. My unorthodox presentation, amateur status, and lack of mathematics also met with distain.

I was bitterly disappointed but Anna, as always, came out with a perfect comment at the right time. "David, in the greater scheme of things recognition doesn't really matter."

Anna, the Twins,
Sam and Becky

Ondine, Lulu, Dadn,
Jessica, Rebecca, Sam,
and Josephine

The School Run

Daisy training her pups

Steven & Shane's Wedding

Lulu outside Bess

Peter Hewitt

Tor Fosnaes

Chapter 25
Broken Home

"It's better to make many women happy than one woman miserable!"

Michael Ash

My mind wasn't constantly occupied with the physics. I had chores to do like hanging out the washing, doing shopping and being on hand to help Anna whenever she needed it.

I had a capacity to leave the work mid sentence when Anna called, then go back and pick it up, half an hour or even a day later, as though it had never been put down. I often wondered if maybe the work already existed in some shelf of my mind and I just tapped into it.

My other task, in 1984, was to take the children to school every morning to give Anna an opportunity to meditate. After dropping off the older ones I took Ondine into the park to push her on the swings. That is when I fell from grace.

A very attractive young woman brought her toddler to play on the swings every morning. Ondine and the little girl became friends and I befriended the mother. On rainy days I took Ondine back to her little friend's house to play. That's when her mum and I began to play too. Anna was pleased with the time I gave her every morning, but while she knew Ondine had a new friend, she didn't know I had a new friend too.

People make excuses but for me there were no excuses. If Anna gave the children more attention than me I had only myself to blame; I shouldn't have given her so many! The truth is I wanted both pudding and pie. I had a beautiful wife whom I loved more than ever before and I had a gorgeous girlfriend who I loved as well. It was irresistible fatal attraction, combined with the stupidity of thinking I could get away with it! I was in the prime of my life, in full creative seminal flow. A stronger man might have stopped himself but I had a weakness for women and I didn't want to stop; I was having too much pleasure to face the thought of the pain I might cause.

My next crime against Anna came in the form of another female; a Jack Russell terrier called Daisy. I bought her as a pup at a pet shop without consulting Anna and made sure the children were with their mother when I opened the 'surprise box'. Then, of course, there was no hope of returning the puppy to the pet shop.

Daisy was a born killer. She would slaughter anything smaller than herself and because we had chickens in a run at the end of the garden, her favourite quarry was chickens. Daisy was obsessed by the hens. She would sit and watch them through the fence all day, studying their every move; occasionally running up and down in a feign chase.

One sad Sunday we visited friends of Anna on a farm near Chichester. Their boy Anthony was planning to be a vet and was in the middle of a chicken breeding project for his GCE A' levels. He had rare breeds of bantam hens and cockerels in several coups with less valuable birds wandering loose. Anthony was coming close to completing a series of genetic experiments. Everything depended on the next clutch of chicks, he explained, as we were admiring his beautiful birds. The children were especially delighted and it was a real joy to watch Anthony explaining his project to Becky and the twins. I locked Daisy in the Morris Traveler when we went in for tea leaving a small window open for ventilation.

It was a mystery how the little bitch wriggled out of the tiny window but the carnage that greeted us after tea was horrendous. Daisy didn't bother with the fowls wandering loose. She headed straight for the coups where the irreplaceable hens and cocks were trapped. Like a fox, she dispatched the lot. We found her triumphant, soaked in blood, surrounded by decapitated prize chickens.

Anthony disappeared. He was later found in a field, lying on the furrows beating the clods with his fists, sobbing his heart out. We could never make it up to Anthony. Daisy was moved to a new home making room for me in the dog-house. My girlfriend was pregnant!

The first three weeks after I broke the news on Anna – who was also pregnant - were hell. I deserved nothing less. Then I managed to persuade my girlfriend to visit her. It took a lot of courage for her to go round and confront my wife especially when Anna was understandably ready to ring her neck. But then something extraordinary happened.

Anna saw my girlfriend from the kitchen window. She then stepped out of the back door with grace and dignity and greeted her with a kiss! The anxiety in my girlfriend's face was replaced with joy and the kindness was reciprocated with a long hug. From that moment on the two mothers became friends. Anna told me afterwards she had been full of anger but as she looked out the window she saw only a mother. Compassion went from her heart to the other and in an instant the hate was replaced with love.

I supported Anna at the birth of Lulu on 9th of October 1985 and Anna supported my girlfriend at the birth of Lulu's half sister Lily on January 20th 1986. Anna never bore animosity toward Lily. She treating her as she did her own. Anna was an angel and the two girls, now grown women, have retained a deep bond of love. However, my behaviour irreparably damaged my marriage to Anna and so, though we remained friends, we separated.

I never blamed Anna for kicking me out; I had stretched her beyond her elastic limits. A fool is a fool for a while, until life catches up. I moved into a bed-sit with my typewriter and got on with life as best I could, then after three weeks of bathing my aching heart in beer, I decided to leave Worthing and move in with Peter.

Peter Hewitt had attended my presentation on the physics of the vortex at the 1987 Festival of Mind Body and Spirit in London and afterwards approached Sir George Trevelyan, who introduced my lecture.

I was speaking to someone else when Sir George interrupted my conversation with some urgency. Pointing to Peter, he exclaimed, "Meet that man!"

I introduced myself and in a measured tone Peter spoke of a profound experience he had in his heart while I was speaking. He was certain, from his study of history and philosophy of science at Cambridge, that I had a valid interpretation of physics and he felt he was destined to work with me on it.

Peter was living alone in a detached London house in Notting Hill Gate and had started editing a draft of a book I was writing called *Science of the Gods* (subsequently published by Gateway Books) Having worked as a journalist Peter was confident he could help me write my book. He was delighted when I offered to move in and work with him on the project.

We were together for two and a half years and Peter was very generous and caring toward Anna and the family as well as me. He had his property on the market when I moved in and within three months it was sold. From the proceeds I received a monthly allowance so I was able to provide for Anna, buy her a decent car to replace the clapped out Morris and pay the rent on the large country house on the edge of Dartmoor where, she settled with Peter's Steinway grand. Anna had decided to start a new life in Devon and put our children into the Rudolf Steiner School at Dartington. There she found new friends and eventually a new husband.

Peter also lent me cash to invest in a cottage in Padstow, Cornwall. He said I could enjoy the cottage for a year then he would sell it to recover his money and I could keep any profit from the sale. The cottage was enjoyed to the full by family and friends. Stephen and his new wife Renata used it for their honeymoon, and I used it frequently for holidays and weekends with the children.

Anna never bore a grudge. Not only did she allow me to stay for weekends to be with the children on Dartmoor, she even joined us in the cottage for one of the holidays; at the time not realizing the extent of financial benefit she would receive from it. Then I met my Hillary, my second wife to be and we had a wonderful time together in the cottage just before it was sold.

1987 - 88 was a boom period on the UK property market and the entire village of Padstow was listed which further increased the value of the cottage. Peter sold the place just before the market crashed and gifted me the profit which extended the period I could provide for Anna and the children as they settled in Devon.

Peter had moved from London into a house in Long Sutton, Somerset where we continued to work together on the book and develop the vortex physics. While I was in Somerset, Pa and Ma moved into the annex of a spectacular property Peter and Muriel had bought with Steven on the North Coast of Cornwall.

Though retired, Pa never rested. He was working on a number of projects, one of which he called *Radiarc.* Pa had bought lengths of large and small bore copper pipe from a local builder's merchant and placed the small pipe inside the large, separating one from the other with plastic spacers. He then soldered a length of wire to the inner pipe and dug the contraption into the ground and the length of wire he then ran round the house.

When I visited him he explained what his device was and how it worked. He said a lot of illness came from energy fields in and under peoples' homes; especially under their beds. The wire, he told me, acted as an aerial and the copper pipe as earth. The arrangement of one pipe inside another acted as a capacitor which, through the wire attached to it, drew away the damaging electromagnetic fields running under the home and made it safe to live in. Pa called this branch of his medicine, *Geopathology.*

Another invention was his health computer which consisted of a plate with metal pads for the fingertips. We placed our fingers on the pads which Pa had connected to a device he made to measure their resistance to electricity. By measuring each finger relative to a standard he calculated the health of the organ it was related to according to the principles in Chinese medicine.

Pa was also working out the ratio of protons and neutrons in every type of atom known to man. From his findings I was able to develop a much better understanding of the atomic nucleus and nuclear binding. Most significantly through his work on the nucleus, Pa drew my attention to the neutron. "Keep your eye on the neutron, David, that is the most important particle in the atom for you," he predicted.

Chapter 26
Vindicating Pa

"Don't give them a nut to crack; crack their nut."

Michael Ash

Toward the end of our time together in Long Sutton Peter began to lose confidence in me. He and Anna had become lovers. Although I was in support of their relationship it engendered in Peter a degree of contempt for me.

I came into the kitchen one morning to find Peter sitting at the table surrounded with books. One was open in front of him. He waited until I had made a cup of tea before making a pronouncement.

"David, your account for the neutron cannot be true. I have it here in this book." Peter declared in triumph, reading out loud what he had discovered.

In the book it said the neutron could not be an electron bound to a proton because if that certainty in the position of an electron were applied to the uncertainty principle developed by Werner Heisenberg then electrons would be chasing round in neutrons with velocities up to 99.97% of the velocity of light.

I was silent over breakfast and for the rest of the day. Peter left me alone to tackle the problem. If my account for the neutron was wrong my theory would collapse and with it his involvement. He was looking for an excuse to pull out.

I had never been happy about the principle of uncertainty developed by Heisenberg because of the way it was used in quantum theory and because Einstein despised it. Einstein was known to have argued with Heisenberg through the night reducing the younger man to tears. Einstein had described his principle as: *A real witch's calculus so ingenious in its great complexity as to be impossible to prove wrong.*

Even though Einstein was the true father of quantum theory, Neils Bohr was the driving force behind its development. Bohr was a powerful and charismatic Danish physicist who received the Nobel Prize for explaining the atom with quantum theory and he favoured the younger minds entering the scene. They displaced Einstein at the pinnacle of physics and Bohr encouraged Heisenberg to use his principle to develop a new branch of quantum theory called 'quantum mechanics'.

Instead of heeding Einstein's warning, physicists throughout the world put their trust in Bohr and Heisenberg. The uncertainty formula was a mathematical delight. The numbers worked even though the quantum mechanical theory was crazy – that particles could borrow energy from the universe as though it were a bank!

Einstein fell out of mainstream quantum physics in the 1920's. Then in the 30's James Chadwick discovered the neutron at the Cavendish Laboratory in Cambridge and Adolf Hitler rose to power in Germany. Heisenberg became the top physicist in Germany and headed the Nazi attempt to build an atomic bomb. Einstein was the Jew that fled Europe for America and wrote the historic letter to President Roosevelt that initiated the American development of the bombs used on Hiroshima and Nagasaki.

The neutron was the deadly detonator of the chain reaction that released the awesome power of uranium on the Japanese cities. It was now about to turn on those that would use it in the creation of weapons of mass destruction.

In his published lectures the American physicist Richard Feynman said: *"If your theories and mathematics don't fit the facts then it is your theories and mathematics that are wrong."*

The facts were that a neutron could be formed out an electron and proton. It had the sum mass of an electron and proton and after a few minutes outside of the atom it would fall apart into an electron and proton. The theories and mathematics that denied the neutron as an electron captured by a proton didn't fit the facts!

Later I would tell the story of a mad professor of puddings who had a thing against plum pud. Because he was President of the Royal Society of Puddings he used his great power and influence to convince the world of cake makers that when plums were baked in a pudding, due to the interaction of a weak cooking force the plums were transformed into cherries and the pudding into a Black Forrest Gateaux.

That was my satire on the stupid theory in physics that due to the interaction of a weak nuclear force, when electrons collide with protons they don't just hang in there like plums in a pud but the electron and proton disappear and the neutron, like a Black Forrest Gateaux, appears as a totally new particle to take their place.

For years I could never understand why sensible scientists, throughout the world denied the truth about the neutron until Peter read from that book. Pa always warned me about how experts would cover up awkward facts and inconvenient truths. Peter had uncovered one of those 'whitewashes' Pa spoke about.

By the time Chadwick discovered the neutron the world of physics had come to accept Heisenberg's quantum mechanics and today Heisenberg's principle is beyond reproach. In his inaugural lecture, Stephen Hawking said that because of the Heisenberg uncertainty principle, electrons could not be at rest in the nucleus of an atom. Hawking's book *A Brief History of Time* had just come out and everyone was treating him as though he were God. I now realised he was speaking in support of scientific fraud

The way I saw it was all the evidence suggested that electrons are at rest in neutrons in the atomic nucleus. Because of that evidence Heisenberg's principle was fallacious. No way could electrons be charging about in the nucleus of an atom at the speed of light. They would be a lot heavier if they were and that extra mass has never been measured in the neutron! No, the math and theory didn't fit the facts – and there are more than the three I listed! Heisenberg was wrong and without his 'witch's calculus' the whole infernal system of quantum mechanics would collapse. But that was only the beginning.

Ironically, Richard Feynman developed a system of quantum mechanics, based on Heisenberg's principle which he called QED for 'Quantum Electro Dynamics'. QED has been the most success theory in the history of science according to the scientific method. If the neutron shattered the uncertainty principle and QED collapsed not only would it be the end of quantum mechanics, but the scientific method would go down in the smash. That meant the scientific criteria for truth would be pulverised and anti-spiritual, materialistic science would be dead!

The day Peter tried to prove me wrong I realised the information he had shown me about the neutron could set off the equivalent of a nuclear explosion in science. No wonder there was a 'cover-up' about it. When I spoke to Pa about this later on he said it would be divine retribution if the particle used in science to detonate the atomic bomb were the cause of its demise.

"But you can't be right," Peter spluttered when I broke the news to him, "The uncertainty principle can't be wrong! It's the major pillar of quantum mechanics! Pull that away and quantum theory could collapse dragging science down with it and that is unthinkable!"

For me it was deliciously thinkable. Thanks to his fastidious research Peter had exposed a major flaw in quantum theory. Like Daisy after a prize chicken, I was in for the kill.

"But Peter," I exclaimed, "Without the materialistic criteria for truth we can believe in angels!

"Hey and we could write our next book on the physics of the fairies!" I added laughing but Peter was not amused. He got up and left, slamming the front door behind him.

I was deadly serious. I was certain there was more reason to believe in angels and fairies than in quarks and the virtual particles of quantum mechanics!

Peter and I parted in 1990 and sadly he suffered a heart attack and passed away in January 2004. We had good times together and achieved a great deal. Warm hearted and generous, though we had our ups and downs, he was as a brother to me.

Meanwhile Pa had been vindicated. Everything he taught me from boyhood had proved right. Professional physicists had betrayed humanity. They had used their knowledge to create the most terrible weapons known mankind and rewarded with unlimited budgets by grateful governments were squandering vast sums of money on particle accelerators designed to prove ridiculous theories that Einstein had warned were fallacious. Professional physicists with their lunatic quantum mechanics were no different to the pompous medieval priests postulating how many angels could be stood on the head of a pin.

Pa was right when he said truth was magnetic; it was attracted by love and repelled by money. But Pa's greatest concern was that the mad scientists with their destructive power would lead humanity over the brink, into a nuclear holocaust where radioactive fallout would rain down on us all and make everyone sick. His whole life had been dedicated to concern over the health hazards of radioactivity; the terrible consequence of the neutron.

Pa was in his mid seventies and his health was beginning to fail. With the outbreak of the first gulf war his concerns over the danger of radioactive fallout returned. He started making emergency packs of minerals and tried to rally our support but I could see the hopelessness of his situation. No one was going to take this dear old eccentric seriously neither was I convinced the conflict would go nuclear. But Pa became very frustrated and banged off ever more incoherent faded letters on his outmoded portable typewriter with its worn out ribbon. He was close to the end.

Chapter 27
The End of Pa's Road

I am still with you, I still hear you. I can still answer you. When you need me I am with you and I love you.

Michael Ash

Shortly before I sold the cottage in Padstow I met the love of my life. She was awaiting me in Dartington; a 1968 Bedford house truck. The wild haired owner was sitting on the back step reading a paperback. When I asked for a peep inside Vincent was happy to oblige. She was gorgeous, done out in carved amber pine like a narrow boat. There was everything on board including kitchen, shower and loo. A wood burning stove sat opposite the single berth with a double birth above the driving compartment and pots of flowers adorned a shelf inside the windscreen. An office chair bolted to a steel frame served as the driver seat and a non-attached wicker chair performed as the passenger seat.

While I was viewing her Vincent said she was up for sale at a thousand pounds but no one in the traveling community had offered more than a few hundred. I said I'd pay him twelve fifty on completion of the Padstow sale if he could make a number of changes to suit my needs. Two months later I was converted as a born again hippie free to travel the new age road. But Bess, as I called her, wasn't the only one to convert me!

One weekend I took Sam, Ondine and Lulu away with me in Bess to the North Coast of Cornwall. We had just parked up in Crackington Haven when there was a knock on the door. I opened to three faces eager for a view and invited them in for tea. There was a gorgeous red head called Kate who turned out to be a premie and another vivacious girl with her husband. She introduced herself as Veronica and announced that they were born-again Christians. Sensing trouble I settled into 'satsang' with Kate and left them to my children who were fixing the tea. That was a fatal mistake.

Veronica and her husband said to Sam, Ondine and Lulu that we were welcome to go back with them to their bungalow near Brentor, on the North edge of Dartmoor. My conversation with Kate was interrupted by a chorus from the kitchen. "Please, Dadn, please can we go back with them!"

Fumbling for an excuse I mumbled that the children had to get back for school. I was shot out of the sky by an Ondine missile, "But Dadn we don't have to be home until Sunday evening," and finished off with Lulu ground-shot, "Please Dadn please, we really want to go!"

I asked the visitors to leave for a few moments while I discussed the matter with my children as an immediate return to Devon was not scheduled. Nothing worked; even the promise of Mars bar sandwiches couldn't dissuade them. In our democracy I was outvoted three to one.

Dismissing thoughts of infanticide, I fired the engine and moved Bess out of the Haven and up the hill after Veronica and her husband. We drove toward Launceston then through Lifton and onto the moor.

After supper my little darlings were tucked up for the night by Veronica and I was left alone to fight a hard head opponent from her chapel. The terms of engagement were simple. If I lost the theological debate I had to convert.

I was knocked out in the first round when I agreed that the Bible was the Word of God. I fought on but to no avail. With a superior knowledge of the Bible every argument I put forward was defeated by my initial concession. By 2:00 a.m. I was exhausted and agreed to convert in the morning.

I looked in on the three little angels sleeping soundly before crawling off to my bunk in Bess. On the way past the kitchen Veronica handed me a cup of tea. Her face was radiant with joy, "I'm so happy, you are my first convert."

It was a sunny Sunday morning in Veronica's garden where I accepted Jesus as my saviour. Sam, Ondine and Lulu were looking on, watching me stew as in some Hottentot pot.

After lunch we went to the moorland chapel to worship with my newfound congregation. After the service I was sitting opposite Veronica in the side room where she recounted her own conversion to the Lord. Her skirt was riding high on her thigh when she said she had been very naughty before she found God. I plunged from grace as I dearly wished she hadn't been saved!

Hillary couldn't believe I would go through with conversion to charismatic Christianity but my integrity demanded as I had been defeated in the debate I had to accept my fate so I drove up to Crackington Haven the following weekend and accepted baptism in the sea by Veronica and her husband. With Veronica in a leopard skin bathing suit it was a gorgeous immersion. Afterwards, with a head full of adulterous thoughts threatening my salvation, I drove across to Widemouth Bay to see what Pa had to say on the matter.

A beaming bewhiskered smile greeted me, eyes twinkling with amusement over the ever presiding reading glasses. Ma set the oven to roast a chicken as the grand old man got out his Bible and a bottle of whisky, "David lets do some Bible study!"

As I watched my father settle into his chair I had a sneaking suspicion Sunday school with him was going to be a lot more fun than with the mob on the moor. Rolling the spirit back on his tongue Pa opened at the first verse of Genesis and read aloud: *In the beginning God created the heavens and the earth.*

"If the Bible were the Word of God which would you take as infallible truth, this King James version I have here or the original Hebrew texts from which it was derived?"

"Obviously the original Hebrew," I replied.

"In the original Hebrew," Pa continued in a measured tone, "It was written: *In the beginning elohim created the heavens and the earth.* Are you aware of what the word 'elohim' means?"

"No!" I had to confess.

"What, the nuns never taught you that?"

"Pa I was only little," I flushed.

Pa was beaming. "In Hebrew," he said with deliberation, "Elohim means the gods."

"Aha," I exclaimed, "That's why in Genesis God speaks in the plural!"

"Absolutely," said Pa pulling on his whisky. "*Let us create man after our own image...*" he read aloud from the Bible.

"Originally the Hebrews believed in many gods not just one God. You should have enlightened those born again Christians that the Bible is the word of the gods."

"That means I've become a born again Pagan," I howled!

Pa had armed me with a veritable Excalibur to ward off onward Christian soldiers. The problem was it had come too late; I now numbered in their ranks.

"I have something else to teach you about God," said Pa, as he thumbed through the Holy pages to the Gospel of John. I loved Pa's economic style. Typically he got straight to the point and found the answers to my dilemma in the very first verse of each book he opened. He read, *"In the beginning was the word and the word was with God and the word was God."*

He closed his Bible and stared at me for a moment over his half rims, savouring his words; "Word is sound, sound is vibration, and vibration is energy, so David the first verse of John's gospel could be written: *"In the beginning was the energy and the energy was with God and the energy was God."*

Pa took another pull on his whisky and deliberated, "If you do believe the Bible is the word of God you are bound to believe that God is energy."

"Pa you're a genius, you've just defined God!"

"Not me, St John!"

"Wow, that single verse in the Bible reconciles science and religion. Pa you're brilliant! I always imagined God as separate to the Universe," I exclaimed, suddenly seeing the light, "but come to think of it, God is neither created nor destroyed and energy is neither created nor destroyed. Everything is of God and everything is of energy. God is everywhere and energy is everywhere. I'm beginning to see your point Pa, God didn't create the Universe; God is the Universe!"

"So it would seem!" Pa concurred, downing the last of his whiskey.

That was last profound discussion I had with my father. Months passed before I saw him again and by then his mind was preoccupied with setting twigs at the high tide mark. He was taking meticulous measurements to see if there was any evidence of sea levels rising due to global warming.

As always he anticipated popular concerns. But it wasn't global warming that finished Pa, it was a winter freeze.

One bright and sunny but freezing Saturday morning in February 1991, I had promised to drive from Dartington in Devon, where I was based, to Bude in Cornwall. I said I would take Pa to a talk he was giving at an alternative health gathering in the town but I couldn't start Bess. The low temperatures had killed the charge on my battery so I took it to a farm and put it on a twenty-four hour recharge. I trudged through the frost to a phone and rang Ma. She said Pa was OK. He had gone to Bude in a taxi.

On Saturday evening I was with Hillary when the phone rang. It was Ma. Pa hadn't returned from Bude and a rescue had been launched in an attempt to find him. She told me she was with Mary and Peter and Richard were out on the search but she knew somehow that Pa was gone.

On Sunday morning a forlorn figure was spotted, from a helicopter, on the cliffs at Widemouth Bay. It was Pa huddled in his sheepskin coat. He was dead.

Later in the morning, someone on the search team found Pa's briefcase on the beach at the bottom of the cliff. He had obviously climbed a path to the spot where he was found lying in the grass facing, not out to sea, but back at the cliff. Richard explained he had been with Pa to that spot on a number of occasions to look for peregrine falcons that nested on the cliff. Peter suggested Pa must have walked back from Bude along the beach and climbed up to watch the falcons and fallen asleep; as was his habit when he went walking on the cliffs.

Allowing for the time it would have taken him after his talk to walk to that spot from Bude it would have been late afternoon. The sun would have gone down and with plummeting temperatures Pa must have slipped away in his sleep. Pa often said to us the best way to die was through exposure because you fell asleep all snug and warm and never woke up. It was typical of Pa to die his preferred way.

Pa didn't deliberately take his own life. That was not in his nature. Pa's way was more the way of old people in ancient native tribes who allowed nature take its course in the bitter winter cold as they trekked on their migration.

It was not that Pa chose his time or means of death. He never planned his life so he would not have planned his death. Pa would have been drawn by the opportunity to walk home along the beach on a beautiful sunny day. The cliffs would have sheltered him from the bitter east wind. The winter sun would have been warm on his walk. The decision to climb to a favourite haunt on the cliffs rather than hurry home would have been taken on the spur of the moment. I knew my father well. He would not have thought through the danger of settling and sleeping on a ledge facing east. He would have been preoccupied with the chance of spotting a peregrine and sleep would have overtaken him unawares in his wait for a sighting. Death for Pa was just another step in a life of faith.

I had no regrets. I knew it was not intended for me to interrupt his destiny. My father had been saved from the cruelty of modern medicine that denied people the dignity of departing before they were trapped in slowly dying bodies, lingering for years in living tombs unable to move on thorough natural causes. Pa died in a natural way and I was happy for him to have achieved that.

I drove up to Cornwall as soon as I could start the engine and joined my brothers in digging his grave next to Tim's in St Genny's church yard overlooking the North Cliffs of Cornwall that he loved so dearly. It was freezing cold and we had to cut through rock with a hammer and masonry chisel but there was joy in the work. We laughed and joked with Pa beyond the veil about his hole. We knew he was there with us. We could feel his joy.

As his coffin and mortal remains were carried into the church Barry Musgrave, a friend of the family, glanced up the hill toward the grave. Pa was standing there, alone, silent watching us all. When Barry looked again he was gone.

Pa at the End

Epilogue

As I was working on the early chapters of this book Steven received an email 'out of the blue' from a man in Newfoundland called Tor Fosnaes who sent us this:

At thirteen, life in Steady Brook, then the "fastest growing small town" around, was quiet and bucolic. Summer days were fishing in the Humber River, swimming in Steady Brook, or in my case, working. I think it was 25 cents for a big bucket of peeled potatoes at the local gas station and take-out (you'd probably say petrol station and take-away). There seemed little else to worry over than getting your Grade XI and either going off to university and a professional life or getting a job at Bowater's Pulp and Paper, the backbone of Corner Brook, a city since 1957.

Steady Brook was named for the "steady", a backeddy of shoals on the Humber River and a famous salmon angling location, at its estuary. Steady Brook the community grew up around the pulpwood boom across the Humber. Millions of four foot long pulpwood of all sizes would gather up behind the boom and every now and then the boom would be opened and the lot would float off to Humber Arm and another boom before being loaded into the pulp mill. The boom was made up of 60 foot long 12 inches square British Columbia cedar chained together. We were supposed not to go on the boom but it was a fishing place and we spent hours on the boom throughout the year.

At the very end of the road near the steady, on the bank of the Steady Brook, was a fishing cabin already 25 or more years old into which the Ash family moved. Dr. and Mrs. Ash and my parents Knut and Nina Fosnaes were friends from their arrival.

I don't remember the details but one day, it was rainy and cold, my dad and I carried a pot au feu to the Ash family, your mother was feeling poorly and all the children had colds. When we arrived Dr. Ash was sitting with a small blond four year old child on his knee; the child had pneumonia we were told. Dr. Ash's hands, I noticed weren't actually touching the baby's chest and back yet the baby sat there upright as if he was touching it. The baby was feverish and half asleep, eyes hooded.

As we watched it was apparent to me that a powerful force was emanating from Dr. Ash's hands; it seemed to glow warmly and pulsated slowly. This went on for a few minutes and then he passed the baby to your mother who swaddled it and held on until the breathing eased and the choking cough ceased.

My father asked if he could drive the baby and Dr. Ash to the hospital in Corner Brook but Dr. Ash was convinced (rightly it turns out the next day) the infection was controlled and would recede in a day or so. It was probably another 15 years before healing hands and aura knowledge was accepted by mainstream Canadian society however minimal the extent to which it is now accepted.

I remember being in the presence of the adults and how your father's conversation was always interesting, whether it was about strontium or nicotine. It took another decade before the Age of Aquarius started to bring environmental awareness to the fore of modern society and to the level of knowledge then evinced by Dr. Ash. I remember him talking about his tobacco research work in Ontario and his Six Nations patients; he was concerned by the relationships between economic, social, and medical well being. All this two decades before it was recognized by Canadian society in general.

I recognized Dr. Ash was ahead of his time. I knew immediately that being in his presence was being in the presence of genius. My father was likewise struck by him. The medical community and public of Corner Brook were not so awestruck by his unorthodox ways it seems. I remember one story of a patient's insistence on being given a prescription and Dr. Ash's insistence that prescriptions were unnecessary and overly used and that such happenings would only lead to misery. He saw the looming antibiotic crisis fully 30 years before the rest of society.

Doctors, lawyers, teachers were considered society's leaders in those times and held in great respect by the public. Oddities were just eccentricities but a complete break with conventional practice as exhibited by Dr. Ash was, I guess, unacceptable. That he was the subject of derision by his fellow Corner Brook doctors was known in our family and I remember a couple of conversations between Dr. Ash and my father about this. My father once told me that he and Dr. Ash were "outsiders" in Newfoundland society and would never be fully accepted as equals.

By 1964 when I left home for Memorial University in St. John's to do Pre-Med (dentistry was my goal) the Ash family were long gone from Steady Brook but not forgotten. We often wondered about the family and I believe there was some early correspondence between our fathers. We heard he had taken up a practice on Harley Street but had no details.

My university career was short and sweet, it seems parties and the looming counter-culture of the 60's took more of my attention than academics. In 1966-1967 I taught school for a year in Woody Point, Bonne Bay then went to Labrador City and Sudbury working as a labourer in the ion ore mines. In 1968 I returned to Newfoundland and Corner Brook and was Local News editor for the Western Star. Having had some experience in editing with the university yearbook (Cap and Gown '64 and '65) I seemed to have a natural research, writing and publishing talent, once dubbed "born with a silver tongue" by a colleague and still called "two cents a word" or "hack writing" by me.

In first year university I was introduced to I Ching, Tao Teh Ching and eastern philosophy. Using Dr. Ash as an example of how one didn't have to always be mediocre and mundane I explored alternative ways of thinking and being that I follow to this day. I told people throughout my life of Dr. Ash's profound influence on my life and my beliefs and often wondered aloud to my friends about his fate. His example I used to justify and validate my own growing alternative life style; remember the number of followers of esoterica in 1970's Newfoundland were few and far between; at times I felt it was limited to me alone; in 21st century Newfoundland we are still a paltry few. My personal search for salvation (remember Gautama said we had to "work out our own salvation with diligence") led me from Japanese poetry and Zen practice (which I missed at first) back to the Hinyana, hoping a knowledge of the origins would bring understanding and acceptance. Not grokking the Hinyana took me to the Mayahana practices of Tibet and then a short step from there to China, and by the mid-70's back to the I Ching the Tao Teh Ching. And now I follow the Path as best I can.

Oh, perhaps my life would have been the same without exposure to Dr. Ash, but I don't think so. I have always held his Steady Brook image in my mind. I was surprised and dismayed by the 1963 LIFE magazine article which showed him as a normal, clean-cut, middle-aged man when our subscription copy arrived in our house. Stephen's picture of him in bearded old age sent by e-mail restored my sense of his amazing persona and presence. I am bearded, I tell people since I was born, a decision made because of Dr. Ash who was probably the only contemporary of my parents who actually had a beard. I knew shaving wasn't an option for me from before I had reason to shave.

The radioactive lollipops, strange as it seemed at the time, even with the scientific put downs quoted in the article, were an early venture into what is now homeopathy. I always tell people of Dr. Ash when conversation turns to homeopathy, aromatherapy, and similar therapeutic methods and techniques. He invented it I figure because he was the first I knew about who ever used it.

***

Tor Fosnaes told us it was his mother, Nina, who bought the four poster bed, Apparently the bed was listed as a bundle of sticks and went under the hammer for $25. Tor's parents also bought the Hepplewhite chair and Queen Anne Sofa, and did build the extension to their home to accommodate the pieces and over the years these became a tourist attraction. Tor said while the sofa was gone he still had the bed and the chair which came into his possession a few years ago when his mother died. He has offered these back to us. Steven and Simon are considering a trip to Newfoundland to reconnect with the past.

David Ash Books
Available from
www.snakestone.org

If the Truth Be Known

Supported by compelling evidence, this is a shocking exposé of Western Religions. Who or what is the God they all worship. Now at last you can understand why the world has been wracked for centuries by unending war and violence. Discover the ancient history of humanity and understand the role of evil involving millennia of suffering for mankind. Appreciate a new understanding spirituality that could usher in an era of peace and reconciliation.

The Science of Super Energy

Most people believe in the supernatural, but their beliefs have been repudiated by scientists. However a growing number of physicists believe energy could exist beyond light. Life beyond light could account for claims of the paranormal and the supernatural. Two self-evident laws govern the relationship between the world of physical energy and these worlds of super energy. A place in science appears for many spiritual experiences and traditional religious beliefs.

Physics of The Quantum Vortex

Millennia before Einstein, Indian mystics probed the atom with their minds and saw subatomic particles of matter are vortices of light. The vortex of energy provides a complete, unifying account for physics and a whole new understanding of the Universe. Explaining the entire body of physics in terms of a single principle and successfully predicting the accelerating expansion of the Universe three years before it was discovered, this could be the physics of the third millennium.

Dr Ash & Sons

Copies of Dr Ash & Sons: Amazing Inventions, Crazy Adventures can be obtained on line direct from www.snakestone.org. Discount prices are available on bulk orders for gifts or resale.